# Genesis or Nemesis

*belief, meaning and ecology*

## COMPASS OF MIND

Knowledge is a dangerous thing, as Adam and Eve found out in the Garden of Eden. Yet without it, humanity would not evolve. Knowledge leads to new pathways of understanding, shaping our views of the world and extending our ability to create. Sometimes ways in which to apply knowledge are sought; at others, knowledge itself is enough, for it is said that man is made in the image of God, and, through knowing himself, can know the divine.

The series "Compass of Mind" is founded in this view of an integrated physical, human and spiritual universe. It looks at various ways in which knowledge is discovered and formulated, drawing themes from mystical and esoteric traditions, from the creative arts, and from therapies and broad-based science. For each topic the questions are posed: "What kind of a map of the world is this?" and "What special insights does it bring?" The series title embodies the concept that knowledge begins and ends with mind; a question asked expands into a circle which is both defined and investigated by mind itself.

Authors of "Compass of Mind" titles bring a wide perspective and a depth of personal experience to their chosen themes. Each text is written with clarity and sympathy, attractive to the lay reader and specialist alike. Themes are illustrated with lively, well-researched examples, aimed at revealing the essence of the subject, for these are books which tackle the question of "Why?" rather than "How to?"

Cherry Gilchrist, series editor

# GENESIS OR NEMESIS

*belief, meaning and ecology*

MARTIN PALMER

DRYAD PRESS LIMITED
LONDON

To my father who taught me how to believe
and my mother and godmother who taught
me how to see


First published 1988
Typeset by
Latimer Trend & Company Ltd,
Plymouth
Printed by Biddles Ltd,
Guildford,
Surrey
for the publishers
Dryad Press Limited,
8 Cavendish Square,
London W1M 0AJ



ISBN 0 8521 9780 2

# CONTENTS

## Acknowledgments

I wish to thank the many people who have made this book possible. My special thanks to my colleagues in the International Consultancy on Religion, Education and Culture (ICOREC), especially Barbara Cousins, Pallavi Mavani, Joanne O'Brien, Kerry Brown and Liz Breuilly. To my colleagues and debaters in the WWF International and WWF UK, especially Frank Schmidt, Leyla Alyanak, Ivan Hattingh and Peter Martin—not forgetting Cherry Duggan—who could! To my mother for the idea of the poem and my wife, Sandra for the idea that actually it could be much better if I only would . . . ! To John Baines and Barbara Taylor who invited me to give the Environmental Education lecture which lies behind this book, and to Ruth Taylor for coming to that lecture and still wanting me to write for this exciting new series. And to Cherry Gilchrist who took some rough ideas and breathed life into them. To you all, thanks.

*Martin Palmer, Shrove Tuesday, 1988.*

The cover illustration is by Gila Zur.

# 1

# I came, I perceived, I conquered

"There are no longer any wild places left in the world." With these words a leading mountaineer opened his address to fellow explorers concerned with the environment.

In Sweden 18,000 of the country's 96,000 lakes are dying as a result of acid rain, caused when industrial pollution released in to the atmosphere reacts with the water in the air to form nitric and sulphuric acid.

Because of deforestation and over-use of the land, over 75 million million tonnes of irreplaceable topsoil are lost every year worldwide, reducing many formerly fertile areas to desert.

Currently something in the region of 10,000 species disappear each year, and one in every ten plant species is threatened with extinction in the next twenty-five years.

The catalogue of ecological woes goes on and on. The pollution of the seas; the near extinction of the whales; the destruction of the ozone layer; the loss of entire eco-systems. The evidence of our destructive impact on the earth lies all around us if we care to notice. It is there in the rivers and bays where no-one dares swim any more. It is there in the decaying fabric of our ancient buildings, eroded by air pollution. It confronts us in the starving faces of the dying in Ethiopia and Mozambique. It lies waiting in the arsenals of nuclear destruction and in the almost ageless toxic waste of our nuclear power plants.

Anguish at our destruction of the natural world is captured

in Cecil Rajendra's poem, written in the late 1970s, "All that's gone and been":

*One rock in particular*
*i remember well*
*hippopotamus-humped*
*jutting belligerently*
*into the retreating sea.*

*Ah, if rocks could speak*
*what stories they would tell*
*of all that's gone and been*
*of days of gold and green:*
*that lush fringe of palm*
*and cashew and coconut trees*
*that sash of unsullied sand.*

*Time was when this beach*
*was so rich in cockles*
*a flick of a child's foot*
*would yield a handful.*

*Time is when you scuff*
*the murky sand to find*
*broken bottles, rusty Coca-*
*Cola cans, prophylactics*
*embedded ankle-deep in slime.*

*And time is when concrete*
*and steel conceits of man*
*besiege my placid hippo-*
*potamus-humped friend.*
*(Marks though they be of*
*progress and prosperity*
*yet who can match her*
*rugged uncosmetic beauty?)*

*And yes, at night*
*unable to hold her silence*
*you should hear how*
*with the tongues of waves*
*she roars her protest*

*at the insane passing*
*of all that's gone and been*
*of those days of gold and green.*

(C. Rajendra, *Dove on Fire*, WCC Publications, Geneva 1987)

We are living in an era of the most intensive environmental destruction the world has ever known. At times it seems as if we have a death wish, but what death wish normally involves killing everything around you, as well as yourself? We know that we cannot continue to use the world in the way we do now, but instead of making us change our ways this seems to fuel our desire to make sure we get "our share" now.

It comes as something of a shock to people when you say there are no wild places left. Most of us recognize that we have fouled our immediate environment, but still cling to a fond hope that "somewhere" things are better, or unchanging. The thought that there are no more wild places strikes at that. Is it true? Yes, because there are no places where the influence of humanity is not felt. The wild places that do exist, do so now because we have decided that we do not need them—yet. We manage them to be wild, we permit them to exist. But in the centre of Antarctica you will find pollution, and DDT is to be found in the penguins. In the heart of the great forests you will find loggers and multi-nationals tearing up the areas of these wildernesses which governments have decided are now profitable. On the mountains of the Himalayas you now have to skirt past the mounds of rubbish left by other tour-group "explorers".

The harsh truth is that virtually everything living on this planet is now in our hands, and those hands do not hold or caress but tighten and destroy. We are now mass managers of the rest of creation, because we determine what stays and what goes. Yet the way we are managing shows not a sense of responsibility, but a suicidal rush to destroy the richness of our world. As though caught in some terrible nightmare, we are consuming the fossil fuels, while seeking alternative sources of energy which will leave nuclear waste active for long after our species has either died out or evolved into a new form.

Yet in the midst of this madness voices are raised, traditional ways of life try to speak out for a saner model of existence, and groups struggle to bring to the peoples of the world an awareness of what we are doing. But although we hear the facts, see the films and know in our heads what we are doing, it seems to make little difference to what we actually do. It is as if we, particularly we in the West, are trapped inside a way of life which is doomed to destruction. Like unquestioning acolytes of a new and terrible deity, we appear to be worshipping the source of our own demise, even though we know that it is not right. Again, the Asian poet Rajendra captures this well, using the imagery of Kali, the destructive side of the goddess Mahadeva:

*"KALI AND THE CAVES"*
*(for Gurmit Singh)*

*So much for the old gods*
*So much for their ancient*
*caves, reverence of land,*
*respect for faith, heritage*
*history, beauty, ecology . . .*
*So much for the old gods.*

*Hail the new God!*
*Hail mutant of Kali!*

*Our new God*
*sits atop a skyscraper*
*has a terrible visage*
*speaks in voice of thunder.*

*Our new God*
*eats mountains, forests*
*regurgitates quarries*
*spits motorways, mortar*
*supermarkets, factories.*
*Our new God's*
*chariot is a bulldozer.*

*Ministers of this new*
*God's ministry do not*
*wear saffron robes*

*or clerical collars*
*but bushjackets*
*and sport briefcases.*
*They are all power-*
*ful and always right.*

*So, the new God's voice*
*booming fire and dynamite*
*prevails over the old gods*
*and four hundred and forty*
*million years of history*
*of stalactite and stalagmite*
*are blasted into obscurity.*

*Hail the new God!*
*Hail mutant of Kali!*

(C. Rajendra, *Dove on Fire*, op. cit.)

## What is this, really?

What are we to make of the world? This is a deliberately ambiguous question. For it implies not just a technical question of control, use and management, but also a question of perception. What do we believe the world to be? For all that we do is influenced, shaped and given meaning by the core beliefs by which we operate, even if we are unaware of these beliefs. Nowhere is this issue of core beliefs more important than in relation to how we see the world, what we believe to be its purpose and where we understand ourselves to fit in all of this. From these beliefs spring our actions and our contemplation. From our understanding or our modelling of the world flow our words and deeds. Let us look at what this means, at the difference that core beliefs, as well as other beliefs, make to the way in which we live and treat, use or value, the natural world.

Let me ask you a simple question. What is a fox? This may seem an innocuous question, but I will ask it again. What exactly is a fox? The answer will depend on what you believe. We all know that the fox looks reddish brown (apart from those chameleon-style Arctic foxes) and has four legs. But beyond that, what do we imagine, what does our mind's eye conjure up, when the word "fox" is mentioned?

For some people, the fox is a threat to their livelihood. The fox is a pest to be trapped, poisoned or shot on sight, for fear that otherwise your chickens will disappear. For others, the fox is a symbol of an ancient way of life—the hunt—with all its ritual, ceremony, special clothes and not to forget the drinks. Whereas the chicken farmer makes no particular claims about what the fox feels when it is shot, trapped or poisoned, the hunters seem to believe that the fox enjoys the thrill of the chase, and the possibility of escape. They often use this belief to justify what seems to many others to be rather peculiar, if quintessentially English, behaviour.

Then there is the city-dweller, who enjoys the conveniences of the city but feels a little guilty about the destruction of the natural environment which urban development has necessitated. One night he catches the glow of eyes and a brief sight of an urban fox slipping across a suburban road, and for a moment the fox symbolizes the resilience of nature. For the hunt saboteur, the fox is the innocent victim of blatant human cruelty—a symbol expressive of all the tension and destruction within the human attitude towards the natural world. To the Western story-teller, the fox is a symbol of cunning and craftiness, from the fables of Aesop to Beatrix Potter and beyond!

And which of these is "right"? It all depends on what you believe. All these views are taken from British society. But what of other societies and belief systems? How do they view the fox?

In Hindu society, the fox is viewed as part of the cycle of reincarnation. Each "*atman*"—"soul"—is seen as being a spark of the Divine. This spark is constantly seeking to be reunited with the Divine Oneness. Popular Hindu belief says that each individual *atman* has to pass through some eighty-four thousand different reincarnations before release and reunion with the Divine One are possible. Thus the fox is another *atman* on its path to reunion. It may even be the reincarnated *atman* of a friend or relative. In that case, killing a fox or any other creature, except in self-defence, is foreign to many devout Hindus.

In both China and Japan, the fox is something other—literally. For the fox is seen as a harbinger of evil. Deeply embedded in Chinese and Japanese folklore and faith is the belief in fox spirits. These dwell in the animals, and seek human bodies which they can possess. It is therefore very dangerous to be near foxes or to disturb them. There is another aspect to this fear of foxes. They are said to be able to turn into beautiful young women, who lure unsuspecting men to doom. Rather in the same way as we in the West have linked badgers with TB (in particular in cattle, apparently from infected grass and soil), so in China and Japan the fox, through its spirit woman forms, is believed to spread venereal diseases.

So I ask the question again. What is a fox? And the answer, in terms of what the fox actually means and is seen to be, depends on your lifestyle, beliefs and traditions. What is true is that, were the World Wildlife Fund (now called the World Wide Fund for Nature) simply to launch a universal "save the fox" campaign, they would not receive a rapturous reception from all sides!

## Knowing our need for myths

What we believe about the natural world, as part and parcel of our cosmology, deeply affects what we actually see the natural world to be. By "cosmology", I mean that picture and understanding of the world, the universe and our place within it, which we all have, but which few of us have ever sought or ever could express in words. Perhaps "cosmimagery" would be more apt, as it is essentially images—which few of us could make into one coherent picture—but let's stick to cosmology even if words fail us! Our perception of the natural world is shaped and focused through the lens of faith—and I do not mean by this simply religious or ideological faith, for those who are willing to take up such labels. We all perceive the world through the eyes of belief; some people recognize this and call themselves Christians or Buddhists or Marxists or materialists, while the rest go on as though they did not have beliefs or myths by which they live.

But no-one lives by bread alone. We all need world views,

understandings literally and metaphorically of where we stand, to enable us to continue existing and to have meaning in that existence. Most of us are unaware of the extent to which we are coddled by certain beliefs, which we never critically examine, simply because we do not see them as beliefs. We see them as "how things actually are" or "the way it is"—all signs of the successful operation of beliefs or myths.

Carl Jung wrote: "Man positively needs general ideas and convictions that will give a meaning to his life and enable him to find a place for himself in the universe." (*Man and his Symbols*, Aldus Books, London, 1964). Elsewhere, he puts it even more sharply: religious myth "is one of man's greatest and most significant achievements, giving him the security and inner strength not to be crushed by the monstrousness of the universe". (*Psychology of the Unconscious*, Collected Works, Vol. 7, RKP). Put bluntly, this means that we cannot exist unless we can fence off the unanswerable and make inhabitable and "safe" the cosmic and eternal. That this has been the role of religious mythology is not in dispute. What few seem to appreciate is that modern secular thought has quite neatly created its own myths of meaning, which operate in just the same way. The fundamental need for a position and a meaning for our lives and for our species dominates whatever system of thought we espouse. We cannot exist conceptually without such cosmologies, yet many people are unaware of the values upon which they have founded their structure of meaning.

It is perhaps helpful to examine the ideas held about two basic subjects—time and ourselves. Everyone has beliefs about these subjects, few have ever critically examined them in relation to their own world view, and even fewer have examined them with regard to their concept of the meaning of creation.

## Time

Time. What is time? Those of us from the West assume time to be, by and large, linear. This means it starts at a definite point and travels on till the end. It goes from A to Z, from Alpha to Omega. The past is not the present and the present is not the future. They are linked but distinct. To this, many of us have attached an idea that things progress as time rolls on. This fits nicely with most people's understanding of evolution or of the development of modern society. Fused to this view of time is a belief that we have only this one existence. The linear model rather presumes this, and thus great emphasis is placed on the value of the one existence. Our proverbs and clichés bear witness to this: "You only live once", "Make the most of it; it's the only chance you get". As we shall see later, this emphasis on the linear, on our once-only existence, profoundly influences our attitudes to the natural world and to our role within it.

But there is another model of time: the cyclical one. In this model, found amongst the faiths of Hinduism, Buddhism and other religions such as Sikhism and Jainism, there is no definite starting-point to life. There is no act of creation. Nor is there a final end, such as the linear model posits. Instead, there is a wheel of life which has neither beginning nor end. In this model of time, all things exist in a cyclical way. Within all life there is a spark of the Divine. This spark is what gives life to the physical forms which appear to us as different people or species. Death is thus the releasing of the divine spark from one particular physical form, in order that it may be reborn in another and thereby continue its progression through the different levels of existence until it is reunited with the Divine. Even then it will be reborn again, at some stage. In this model, living beings, worlds, universes and even the gods themselves are subject to birth, death and rebirth. There is no first origin and no final end. Each individual existence or life is important, but is not the only opportunity for living. Therefore, there is not the same emphasis on success in this particular life as there is in the linear model.

## Who are we?

The second fundamental belief is in ourselves. What do we believe we are? Are we, as in the Western model, whether religious or secular, the main fruit and purpose of creation/evolution? Or are we, as in certain Eastern traditions and particularly in certain indigenous belief systems, just part of a greater whole, with certain powers and responsibilities, but only within the context of that whole? The role we believe we have, the significance we believe we have, are crucial to our relationship with the rest of life. There is great diversity, as we shall see, within each of the positions outlined, but the main divide is still an important one.

Let us look at a number of key belief systems in their broadest details; at how they see the issues of time and humanity's status. How do these beliefs manifest themselves in basic attitudes to the natural world?

## Traditional Chinese religions

One of the oldest and most consistent belief systems is that which is commonly referred to as traditional Chinese religion. This term covers a vast spectrum of time and, in some instances, an almost impenetrable mass of deities and divinities, beliefs and customs, rites and rituals.

### SHAMANISM

The roots of traditional Chinese religion lie in what could arguably be called the earliest world religion—shamanism. The shaman is one who can communicate or make a link between the spirit world and this world—a form of medium. Through such mediums certain powers including healing, divination and revelation are made available.

The world of shamanism (which is still practised today in parts of China, Japan, Indonesia and Siberia) is a magical and highly charged one of trances and apparently superhuman feats such as walking on burning coals or being pierced by sharp instruments. But at its core lies a basic desire to be in tune with and responsive to (or possibly in some sort of control of) the natural forces around us. Our world is seen as but a part of the various levels of the true world. Actions in this, material, and thus lesser world of ours, have to accord with the greater rhythms of the other levels—especially the spiritual one. These rhythms are seen as truly natural, and the shaman seeks to be a bridge between our world, with its faults, and the spiritual and thus more "natural" world.

This shamanistic background provided the rich soil in which traditional Chinese religion grew. The key figures of Chinese mythological history (traditionally set in the middle of the third millenium BCE*) are all shamanistic in actions, clothing and attributes: they include Fu-hsi, Shen-nung and Huang-ti—members of the groups known as the Three August Ones and the Five August Emperors. Semi-shamanistic, semi-rulers, these figures are credited with teaching humanity all that was necessary to begin civilisation. The fundamental shamanist beliefs served China well until the beginnings of statecraft and the arrival of Confucian thinking at the end of the fifth century BCE.

## CONFUCIANISM

Confucius sought to establish rules against which standards of human behaviour could be precisely gauged. Hierarchy provided the measure, and the famous Chinese system of respect arose. The woman must respect the man; the younger brother, the elder; the sons, the father; the subject, his ruler. Confucius had little time for the spiritual world. For him it existed, but to enter into debate or speculation concerning it was a waste of time and ultimately pointless with regard to how to run your life. Needless to say, this had little effect upon the shamanistic practices of the ordinary people.

It is in the development of the two other major expressions of organised Chinese religion that the Chinese understanding of the natural world arises in its vitality. These are Taoism and Buddhism.

## TAOISM

Taoism is divided in Chinese into *Tao Chia*, meaning School or Philosophy of the Tao, and *Tao Chiao*, meaning Religion of the Tao. The term "Tao" is usually translated "Way". At the core of both approaches lies the concern for a proper harmony with nature.

In Tao Chia, philosophical Taoism, the old shamanistic concern of relating this world to the rhythm of nature—the spiritual world—was transformed into a highly sophisticated, intellectual and meditational approach. The extraordinary

*BC and AD are Christian terms signifying acceptance of Christ as Lord. It has therefore become customary in interfaith works to use the terms Before the Common Era (BCE) and Common Era (CE) to denote these periods of time but without a confessional element.

book, the *Tao Te Ching*, supposedly written in the sixth century BCE by Lao Tzu, teaches that the Tao—the Way—is the Way of Nature, the true Way of the Universe. It is a balance of opposites which achieve a harmony. Those who are wise enough to know, understand and follow the Way will find that life will carry them effortlessly. Those who seek to dominate nature, or struggle to impose their will upon it, will find that they are broken or cast aside. The following verses from the *Tao Te Ching* illustrate much of what has just been said:

Chapter 10: *Produce and provide a good environment;*
*Produce but do not possess.*
*Act but do not control.*
*Raise but do not harvest.*
*This is called Profound Teh.*

Chapter 17: *How invaluable are the words,*
*'When an accomplishment is achieved and the task finished*
*People say it was only natural.'*

Chapter 22: *Yield, and become whole.*
*Bend, and become straight.*
*Hollow out, and become filled.*
*Exhaust, and become renewed.*

*Small amounts are obtainable;*
*Large amounts are confusing.*
*Therefore the Sage embraces the Oneness of the Tao*
*And becomes a guide for the whole world.*

Chapter 25: *'Great' can be described as going ever onward.*
*'Going ever onward' can be described as going far.*
*'Going far' can be described as returning.*
*Hence, the Tao is great.*
*Heaven is great, earth is great, and mankind, also, is great.*
*There are four phenomena of greatness in the universe,*
*and mankind is one of them.*
*Mankind follows the ways of the earth,*

*The earth follows the ways of heaven,*
*Heaven follows the ways of Tao,*
*And Tao follows the ways of Nature.*

(*Lao-Tzu: "My words are very easy to understand"*, Man-jan Cheng, published in Chinese, 1971, trans. Tam C. Gibbs, North Atlantic Books, Richmond, California, 1981)

Tao Chiao, the religion of Tao, arose during the first to the second century CE and is a much more direct continuation of the old shamanistic customs. The key figure in this was Chang Tao Ling, who, in the early second century, founded a sect or cult of magical healing, spiritual disciplines and occult practices. The roots lie in shamanism, but to the old stock Chang brought the newer element of personal salvation and the possibility of achieving Heaven through immortality. It is this later form of popular, magical healing Taoism which is still widely practised amongst the Chinese today. A glimpse into this highly complex world affords a chance to assess its perception of our place in nature and some of the ethical considerations which arise.

The highest goal of a Taoist is to become a *hsien*—an immortal. This is one who through selflessness, charity, study, meditation and physical exercises is able to gain both spiritual and physical immortality. Such a person fully lives and is the "Tao", the way of nature, and therefore is able to become part of the continuous flow of nature which, being cyclical, is never-ending. To become part of nature one must live fully in accord with it, recognising both one's relationship with all other forms of living beings and one's place with them as part of a wider pattern and purpose. This is captured in the following tale.

In the fifth century CE there lived a famous doctor and Taoist master called T'ao Hung Ching. He studied the natural world and wrote many volumes about medicine. He longed for hsienship—immortality. One day, to his astonishment, one of his students suddenly achieved immortality. It was unheard of for a student to precede his master in this way. T'ao Hung Ching sought an answer from the gods. "It is quite simple," they replied. "In your books of medicine you use parts of animals, thus causing them distress or even death to provide the ingredients you require. This is totally against the teachings of the Tao. Your student realised this, and in his writings he mentions only herbs and minerals. Thus he was able to achieve immortality." Duly chastened, T'ao Hung Ching rewrote every one of his books, removing all use of animal ingredients, and shortly after he finished he achieved immortality.

## BUDDHISM

Buddhism first began to have some impact on China in the first century CE, although, as a "foreign" religion, and, in particular, one which advocated celibacy and poverty in the monastic ideal, it took many centuries to be accepted as a valid part of Chinese religious life. Confucianists opposed it because it seemed to sacrifice the hierarchical norms of this life—respecting your parents, supporting them in their old age, by getting married, having children, continuing the family name—for the chance of a better rebirth through becoming a monk. Confucianism itself remained very quiet about the afterlife, considering that it was difficult enough to instil the notion of duty, let alone deal with metaphysical issues. It does, however, have the practice of ancestor-veneration attached to it. Also, the whole tradition of monasticism—of the Buddhist *Sangha* (community of monks)—was alien to Confucian thought. What Buddhism did offer to the ordinary Chinese was a sense of personal purpose and of salvation. Taoism soon responded by providing its own framework of salvation, that is to say, the elements which brought Tao Chiao into being as discussed above.

Undoubtedly, Buddhism's greatest achievement was to fuse its own teachings with fundamental Chinese concepts. The Chinese belief in two elemental and essentially natural forces known as *yin* and *yang* was retained alongside the Buddhist ideas of *karma*, *samsara* and rebirth. The Buddhist belief is that whatever we do has a consequence, an outcome—*karma*—which has to be worked through. These consequences do not resolve themselves in just one lifetime, but continue to the next, which is in fact caused by the accumulation of *karma*. This wheel-like effect is called the wheel of suffering, or *samsara*. We pass from birth to death to rebirth until such time as we have no *karma*, no "cause" for a further rebirth, whereupon we achieve release.

Buddhism brought as well a sense that there was a higher

Power in charge of life which was not just the sum total of two elemental forces. *Yin* and *yang* became the natural instruments through which the Divine expressed itself and through which, in part, the world was kept ordered. Chinese Buddhism taught, therefore, that whilst certain aspects of life were fixed by cosmic, natural forces such as *yin* and *yang*, there was also a greater Power which acted apart from, or in a higher, perhaps, more moral way than, the forces of nature. This meant that there was still space for acts of compassion and kindness to effect change. Compassion is seen in Chinese Buddhism as one of the basic attributes of the Divine, and thus any act of compassion, not least to the natural world, by an individual, brings forth a response from the Power behind all things—the Divine. A short story will perhaps show how this understanding and cosmology work.

There was once an old monk who was very skilled in the art of physiognomy. He had a young servant called Sung Chiao. One day he looked into the boy's face and saw clearly that the forces of *yin* and *yang*, the five elements and the other cosmic forces present in the boy's face foretold death within the next month. Being a compassionate man, the monk did not tell the boy of his impending doom, but instead told him to take a month off and to return to his family for a holiday.

The boy set off for his village many miles away. Some days into his journey he came across a stream swollen by flood water. Trapped in the middle of the rising waters was a colony of ants. Moved by compassion, the boy made a bridge of straw, across which the ants swarmed to safety. The boy travelled on. Well over a month later the old monk was astonished to see the boy returning. He quizzed him carefully about what he had done since he had left. When he heard of Sung Chiao's act of compassion, he knew that Buddha had extended the boy's life as a reward. Compassion deserves compassion.

## YIN AND YANG

Key to the whole system of Chinese traditional belief is the concept of *yin* and *yang* and the tension of harmony which they generate. These primeval forces are direct opposites: light/dark; male/female; hot/cold; dry/wet; and so on. They are the fundamental forces of the universe which maintain order through being locked in conflict. So the Chinese model of the cosmos is dynamic and volatile, for harmony is not the absence of conflict, as it is so often seen to be in the West, but the balancing of powers which have the potential to destroy each other by mutual resistance or attack.

Into this dynamic, volatile model comes humanity. There is no place here for a hierarchy of beings which has the simplest creature at the bottom and humanity as the summit of the pyramid, and God or the Ultimate as both the foundation stone and the final pinnacle of the entire edifice. Such a tiered model could not function in a world which is seen as a cosmic "either/or". In the *yin/yang* world of the Chinese, all creation has elements of these two forces within it. Thus all creation is affected by these forces as they struggle for supremacy. In this view, all creation is equal, because the same two forces operate within everything. The only difference is in the scale of the being, or in the capacity of the being for consciously understanding the forces within.

This world view, this cosmology, leads to two apparently contradictory responses in Chinese thought and mythic imagery. The first is the rather wonderful story of how human beings were created. In the West we have all sorts of tales which give us great standing (including the ego-building popular versions of evolution as survival of the fittest). The Chinese story is slightly different. According to this, after the two primal forces of *yin* and *yang* came into being, they created the giant P'an Ku. He set to work on the earth, shaping it, building it up and giving it much of its basic form which we know today. Yet it was still "unalive". At last, exhausted by his Herculean labours, P'an Ku died. From his body flowed forth life. His blood became the rivers and seas; his hair formed the forests and woods; his flesh became the soil; his voice became the thunder. And from the vermin on his body came forth human beings! What an ignominious start!

The second picture is, at first glance, very different. In traditional Chinese thought, there is a triad of forces: Heaven, Earth and Humanity. This would appear to elevate humanity, and yet it is not really so. In fact, the position of humanity is one of onerous responsibility to maintain the distance between Heaven and Earth, the balance between *yin* and *yang*. This means that humans have to find their fulfilment in being subservient to the two forces, and thus in helping to sustain the balance within nature which makes all life possible. All that humans do has to be seen in relation to greater forces, which will crush humanity if the balance is upset.

This role is beautifully personified in the ancient annual ritual which only the Emperor, the Son of Heaven, could perform. Each year he went to the Temple of Heaven to offer a sacrifice on behalf of the people. The sacrifice had one purpose: to restore the balance of the triad of Heaven, Humanity and Earth, through making amends for all the actions of human beings which had disturbed the balance of *yin* and *yang*. In popular thought, floods and fires, famines and military invasion were the direct consequence of the sins of the people, both against each other and against the natural order. In making his sacrifice, the Emperor accepted ultimate responsibility for his people's actions, and he was permitted, as the Son of Heaven, to wipe the slate clean and restore the balance of nature.

Essentially, traditional Chinese religion views the natural world as full of forces which are infinitely greater than humanity and of which humanity is but one expression. However, humanity's role is to maintain balance for all life, either through seeking to follow the natural path—the Way or the Tao—or through placating the natural forces. Thus, for the Chinese, any action by human beings which affects the natural world should reflect this attitude of holding the ring. Take, for instance, the way the Chinese traditionally sited and built their homes. We shall look at this in greater detail in Chapter 3, but, briefly, there is an entire art known as *feng shui* which governs the siting and building of a house or indeed of any edifice.

The term *feng shui* means "wind water" and refers to the *yin* and *yang* forces. When the Chinese come to build in a certain area, they do not view the land as inert, but as alive with forces already long established. The art of *feng shui* is to ensure that any addition to the scene by humanity follows the ebb and flow of forces already present and, in certain cases, actually enhances them. Not to pay attention to this brings the risk of disaster falling upon the house and family, as to go against natural forces is to court danger.

A daily ritual in most traditional homes and businesses is to offer incense to the local earth god, upon whom your fortunes—literally—rest. In this simple action there is a whole world of meaning; it expresses respect for the earth, acceptance that you are there on sufferance, and a belief in a spiritual world of which you are but a part (or on which you are even a parasite) and which you must never take for granted.

## Western Christianity

A very different model of the universe and of humanity's role within it is found in Western Christianity. I use the term "Western Christianity" advisedly, for much which we in the Roman Catholic and Protestant world take as absolutely normative in the Christian faith is, in fact, a result of the particular historical background of these two major expressions of Christianity. There is, however, one other major expression—the Orthodox tradition—which differs in many significant ways from the Western form, not least in its working out of the meaning of creation and of the Creator of us human beings.

I am presenting Christianity as a counterpoise to Chinese beliefs and will not therefore draw specific attention to points of radical difference, assuming that the reader will see these for himself. There is no implication that one system is "better" than the other. As will become apparent later in the book, each has its moral, ethical and practical benefits and each its unfortunate and destructive spin-offs. Simplistic games of comparative religion are not what this book is about.

The Judaeo-Christian tradition sees time as linear. Creation has a definite beginning and will have a definite end. Creation is not just the result of natural forces working together, but is a conscious, willed action of God who, in calling the world into being, has given it meaning and purpose. Likewise the ending of time, of the creation, will be an action of intent, not just an accident. Creation, or evolution, is therefore purposeful and intentional. All that exists has meaning for God and, as the catechism of the Roman Catholic Church states, he has created nothing unnecessarily and has omitted nothing that is necessary. Therefore all creation is beloved of God. Unlike in the Buddhist or Hindu model, creation is not part of God and God is not "in" his creation, in the sense of a spark of the Divine being in each living being. But all creation is purposeful to God and, in that sense, sacred.

The Christian tradition shares with its mother, Judaism, a belief that humanity is somehow different from the rest of creation. This is expressed mythically in the Book of Genesis, by humanity being the last thing which God makes; it is created in "the image of God", brought to life through the infusion of God's breath—vitality, allowed to name the creatures and thus to have power over them. As the psalmist puts it in Psalm 8:

*I look up at your heavens, made by your fingers,*
*at the moon and stars you set in place—*
*ah, what is man that you should spare a thought for him,*
*the son of man that you should care for him?*

*Yet you have made him little less than a god,*
*you have crowned him with glory and splendour,*
*made him lord over the work of your hands,*
*set all things under his feet . . .*

(All biblical quotes are from the Jerusalem Bible, first published in 1966)

When God gives power it is always assumed to carry with it a responsibility to God in the way it is exercised. To think otherwise is to assume an immoral or amoral God, and runs contrary to the whole ethos of the Judaeo-Christian tradition. This is reflected in a fine story in the *Talmud*, the Jewish traditional commentaries on the *Torah*, the first five books of what Christians refer to as the Old Testament.

Adam walked on the first day in the Garden. Seeing an apple, he went to pick it, but the tree withdrew its branches so that the apple was beyond his reach. Turning, he saw a peach and drew close to take it: but the peach tree lifted its branches and again the fruit was beyond Adam's reach. The same happened with the vine and its grapes. Then a voice spoke to

Adam: "First till the soil, water and tend the trees, then you may eat of their fruit."

In the Judaeo-Christian tradition at its best, humanity is seen as being a steward of God. As a steward, humanity is given great powers and has the right to use the natural world. But a steward who despoiled his master's property would not be employed for very long. The basic assumption within the Judaeo-Christian model is that "the earth is the Lord's and the fullness thereof". We have it in trust and must pass it on in trust to our children and their children. Humanity is definitely central, but not the centre—for that is God.

The story of Noah reflects humanity's power over nature, the unique relationship with God, and also the responsibility. The first story of salvation in the Bible concerns the salvation not just of human beings, but of all the species of the world. God's purpose is clear. Noah has to undertake the building of the ark for all life, even that which he is not terribly well disposed to save. Because of the evil of human behaviour, God despairs of the world and determines to destroy it. Through the goodness and responsibility of one man, Noah, God is willing and able to save all life. Thus humanity is seen in this, the first passion narrative of the Bible, to be both the active agent of sin and destruction and the primary vehicle of God's salvation.

Genesis 9 pictures the ark grounding on Mount Ararat and all the occupants streaming forth. Then:

> *God spoke to Noah and his sons. 'See, I establish my Covenant with you, and with your descendants after you; also with every living creature to be found with you, birds, cattle and every wild beast with you; everything that came out of the ark, everything that lives on the earth. I establish my Covenant with you: no thing of flesh shall be swept away again by the waters of the flood. There shall be no flood to destroy the earth again.'*
>
> *God said, 'Here is the sign of the Covenant I make between myself and you and every living creature with you for all generations. I set my bow in the clouds and it shall be a sign of the Covenant between me and the earth. When I gather the clouds over the earth and the bow appears in the clouds, I will recall the Covenant between myself and you and every living creature of every kind.'*

Most clearly, the first covenant God makes, according to the Bible, is with all creation, not just with humanity.

Having established the background against which the human drama is performed—namely that of all life and creation being part and parcel of God's purpose—the Old Testament concentrates on the drama of human salvation and purpose, and largely takes as granted the existence and meaning of all other forms of the creation. Humanity is undoubtedly the key element of the dramatis personae in the Old Testament (after God, that is!) Yet there are timely reminders of the value and meaning to God of his whole creation, even of creation without humanity. Take, for instance, the Book of Job. Chapters 38 and 39 of this magnificent book are a paean of praise by God to God, for creation. And it is cited or recited to put humanity, and especially Job, very firmly in its or his place. In it, God revels in aspects of nature which will never be seen by humanity but which are as important to God as any other part. Meaning in nature is not given by humanity's knowledge or use of it. Nature has meaning apart from humanity.

*Then from the heart of the tempest Yahweh gave Job his answer.*
*He said:*

*"Who is this obscuring my designs*
*with his empty headed words?*
*Brace yourself like a fighter;*
*now it is my turn to ask questions and yours to inform me.*
*Where were you when I laid the earth's foundations?*
*Tell me, since you are so well-informed!*
*Who decided the dimensions of it, do you know?*
*Or who stretched the measuring line across it?*
*What supports the pillars at their bases?*
*Who laid its cornerstone*
*When all the stars of the morning were singing with joy,*
*and the Sons of God in chorus were chanting praise?*
*Who pent up the sea behind closed doors*
*when it leapt tumultuous out of the womb,*
*When I wrapped it in a robe of mist*
*and made black clouds its swaddling bands;*
*when I marked the bounds it was not to cross*
*and made it fast with a bolted gate?*

*Come thus far, I said, and no farther:*
*here your proud waves shall break.*

*Have you ever in your life given orders to the morning*
*or sent the dawn to its post,*
*telling it to grasp the earth by its edges*
*and shake the wicked out of it,*
*when it changes the earth to sealing clay*
*and dyes it as a man dyes clothes;*
*stealing the light from wicked men*
*and breaking the arm raised to strike?*
*Have you journeyed all the way to the sources of the sea,*
*or walked where the Abyss is deepest?*
*Have you been shown the gates of Death*
*or met the janitors of Shadowland?*
*Have you an inkling of the extent of the earth?*
*Tell me all about it if you have!*
*Which is the way to the home of light,*
*and where does darkness live?*
*You could then show them the way to their proper places,*
*or put them on the path to where they live!*
*If you know all this, you must have been born with them,*
*you must be very old by now!"*

(Book of Job, 38:1–21)

*"Do you know how mountain goats give birth,*
*or have you ever watched the hinds in labour?*
*How many months do they carry their young?*
*At what time do they give birth?*
*They crouch to drop their young,*
*and let their burdens fall in the open desert;*
*and when the calves have grown and gathered strength*
*they leave them, never to return.*

*Who gave the wild donkey his freedom,*
*and untied the rope from his proud neck?*
*I have given him the desert as a home,*
*the salt plains as his own habitat.*
*He scorns the turmoil of the town:*
*there are no shouts from a driver for him to listen for.*

*The mountains are the pastures that he ranges*
*in quest of any type of green blade or leaf."*

(Book of Job, 39:1–8)

Christianity shares its fundamental beliefs about creation, humanity and God with Judaism. But it differs from that religion because of its profession of Jesus Christ as Lord. Judaism has a linear view of history, with the Messiah heralding the End of Time. Christianity interprets this linear view, of time flowing from the beginning to the end, from Alpha to Omega, in the light of the life, death and resurrection of Jesus Christ. In the coming of Christ, Christians believe the old world and order have begun to collapse. In each person's coming to know the transforming power of Jesus, personal time stops in its tracks and undergoes a revolution whereby the Christian becomes a part of the Kingdom of God—of the New Age. This has led to two main developments or changes: on the one hand, a greater sense of the sinfulness of humanity, because of our constant attempts to deny what we now know to be the will of God; and on the other hand, a belief that things can be changed here and now—that who we were can be changed and a new life be begun in Christ. Because of this, the Christian believes that he or she can share in the promise of the future kingdom of God when, as the Book of Isaiah puts it:

*The wolf lies with the lamb, the panther lies with the kid, calf and lion cub feed together . . . the infant plays over the hole of the cobra; into the viper's nest the young child puts its hand. They do no hurt, no harm on all my holy mountain, for the country is filled with the knowledge of God as the waters cover the sea.*

(Isaiah 11:6–9)

The core teachings of Christianity which arise from this vision of Isaiah's, and the perception which this picture should provide for Christians of how to live in nature, were captured by Father Lanfranco Serrini, Minister-General of the Franciscans, in 1986.

*Through his almighty word, God created all things visible and invisible. He created them freely and wisely to manifest his glory and infinite love. And the Lord God continues to provide for all his creatures in a most generous manner: he unfailingly gives them life and sustains them.*

*Even when men and women disobeyed their Creator and were enslaved by the disharmony they thus introduced into their relationship with God and creatures, the infinitely faithful Lord continued to love them. Indeed God saved humanity by sending his Son, Jesus Christ, who is the Divine Word and the eternal Wisdom made human.*

*In his faithfulness to what he has made and declared to be very good, God the Father sends his life-giving Spirit to renew humanity and the whole earth, arousing in human beings a firm hope in the life of the world to come, a world of justice, peace and harmony.*

...

*But the heart of Christian faith resides in its proclamation of God's merciful fidelity to himself and to the works of his hands. Christians believe that God the Father has not abandoned men and women to their sinful ways but has sent the Saviour to bring redemption and healing to everyone and to all things. . . . They [Christians] maintain that, risen from the dead and ascended into heaven in his glorified humanity, he reconciles all things visible and invisible, and that all creation is therefore purposefully orientated in and through him, towards the future revelation of the glorious liberty of God's children when, in the new heaven and the new earth, there will no longer be death, mourning, sadness or pain. . . . Christians therefore cannot be pessimistic about the future of the world.*

(*Religion and Nature Interfaith Ceremony*, World Wide Fund for Nature, International, 1986, and The Christian Declaration of Assisi, World Wide Fund for Nature, International, 1986)

In the Christian understanding of the redemption of the world by Christ, one can see clearly the central role given to the human race by Christianity, but one can also see that the salvation of humanity takes place within the overall salvation of all creation. Christ is sent to the world by God because, as the Gospel of John says, "God so loved the world that he sent his only begotten Son . . . (Chapter 3:15–16). And St Paul puts very clearly the purpose of Christ's reconciliation of the world with God, in Colossians 1:18b–20:

*As he is the Beginning,*
*he was first to be born from the dead,*
*so that he should be first in every way;*
*because God wanted all perfection*
*to be found in him*
*and all things to be reconciled through him and for him,*
*everything in heaven and everything on earth*
*when he made peace*
*by his death on the cross.*

Sadly, it has to be said that the Church has tended to lose sight of the fact that salvation was for "everything on earth" and has presented the atonement of Christ as basically of significance only to human beings. Yet, throughout the history of the Church, there have been those faithful who have borne witness to a wider sense, both of humanity's responsibility to, and of its place within, nature.

The most famous of these is undoubtedly St Francis. But Christian responsibility to nature is much deeper, and both far more structured and far more ancient, than is shown by the example of one man—even one as remarkable as Francis. The roots of practical Christian ecology—of making use of nature but also seeking to care for and respect it—are to be found in the rules which form the foundation of Western monasticism. The Rule of St Benedict of Nursia (c.480–c.550 CE) saw spirituality and practical husbandry of the land, waters and forests, as part and parcel of the same response of the soul to God. The Benedictine model of use but not abuse of natural resources is now being imitated, particularly by concerned farmers, throughout the world—yet it arose quite naturally for Benedict as a result of his understanding of God's salvationary love for the world in Jesus.

The basic perception underlying Benedictine farming, that the land is a living reality to be stewarded by humanity, came to form the best in traditional Western agricultural attitudes before agri-business took over. The idea of letting the land rest;

of not disturbing wildlife in those fields; of leaving fallen corn and fruits for the animals; and so many other actions which betoken respect for other creatures and aspects of nature on the land, spring from the Judaeo-Christian world view and, in particular, from the practical example set by the humble Benedictines and other monastic communities. The disappearance of these ancient values and perceptions in very recent years is probably one of Europe's greatest ecological disasters, for not only have we lost much of the beauty of our countryside, but whole eco-systems—interlinking species of plants and animals, hills and valleys, which sustained each other—have been disturbed or destroyed.

The concept in Western ecology of "sanctuaries" comes directly from the Christian witness. The idea of a place which violence, force, the sword or even the state or king could not reach and could not violate, is deeply rooted in the Christian Church. The duty of Mother Church to care for and to spare her wayward children was not limited to humans. As early as the seventh century religious sanctuaries for wildlife were being established by holy men; for instance, St Cuthbert, on Farne Island off the coast of Northumberland. Again, this was a simple outworking of Cuthbert's understanding of the natural world which he derived from his faith.

## We are what we think

By looking at Chinese and Western Christian thought, I have tried to show how fundamental beliefs about time, creation, humanity and purpose affect the ways in which people view the world. In a later chapter we shall look at the substantive difference this makes to the ways in which they actually treat the natural world. What I hope has come across is that the very core of our understanding of the world is shaped by beliefs, even if we are not aware that they are beliefs. One could say that perceptions operate at three levels. There are the implicit, unexamined assumptions about the world, ourselves and meaning, which shape us and mould us whether we are aware of it or not. Then there are the explicit outworkings of certain core beliefs, which manifest themselves as ethical codes and moral behaviour. Finally, there are symbolic structures, such as ritual, art and symbols themselves, which help us to express our most fundamental hopes and fears about the world in which we live and reality as we perceive it to be. That there is often a disparity between one level and another is apparently a dimension of human nature. It is essential that we keep the three in creative interaction, for between them they help us see, if we wish, what we hold to be true, what we should do to be true, and what we experience as true.

Sadly, there is usually a great difference between what we say and what we do. In the second chapter I want to look at what can happen to perceptions when they lose their wholeness, or when new and destructive values are grafted on to older traditions without due awareness of what is being done. For the mess which we are currently in, environmentally, is as much a mess of the mind, a perceptual shortfalling, as it is a practical mess of polluted waters, wasted land and vanishing species.

In this chapter I have tried to show how the physical world is interpreted through beliefs and values. These shape not just what we see, and what we believe to be its purpose but also the rights we think we have over the natural world and the role we think we play there. To talk of ecology or conservation of our world without talking about values and perceptions, beliefs and ethics, is to talk nonsense, for as the philosopher Janet Martyn Soskice has so aptly said:

> *Man only deceives himself when he regards his own linguistic constructs as embodying some trans-anthropological truth. Escape to a purer, strictly representational language is not even possible; at most, one can revel in the fact that man, like the spider, spins out of himself the world he inhabits.*
>
> (*Metaphor and Religious Language*, Clarendon Press, Oxford 1985)

Let us therefore recognize the world views we all spin for ourselves and within which we seek to live in mental comfort. For we need them to keep us sane, and without such views we would be unable to function. But there is a danger—a danger of becoming trapped in a world view, a cosmology of which we are not aware but which still shapes and moulds us unbeknown to ourselves. This moulding affects our very thoughts and language, our perceptions and actions, so as to make us victims of our own myths rather than participants or controllers. This becomes crucially important when these unacknowledged, or only partly acknowledged, beliefs begin to destroy the physical world on which we live. It is also dangerous for us if we are operating with beliefs which have lost their roots and have become adversely affected by other values which seem to coincide, but which actually carry us far from the secure foundations which mythologies and cosmologies should provide. It is at this that I now wish to look, and in particular at certain contemporary expressions and developments of older traditions such as Christianity, Buddhism and classical Humanism.

# 2

# Ecological Crisis of the Mind

In the first chapter we looked at how certain fundamental attitudes are derived from the cultural matrix within which we each find ourselves. We are all creatures of myth, dwelling in a half world of reality and a half world of belief, and this is the basis for our understanding of what we care to call reality. This is how we shall always be. People sometimes get very worried, angry or frightened when they realize the extent to which we function and perceive mythologically. Yet there is really no basic reason for alarm—the human mind and, therefore, the human animal cannot function any other way.

We have also looked at how key concepts of what nature is, or rather of what we are in relationship to nature, are the direct corollary of our particular world view or belief. Again, this is how we function and there is nothing particularly surprising or worrying about that. Once we have learnt to stop pretending that we are objective observers and recognize that, in order to look at anything, we have to be standing somewhere to get a perspective, and that "somewhere" is already a position, then we can begin to appreciate the true value and significance of other viewpoints, perspectives and visions.

What is disturbing is the extent to which old, tried-and-tested belief systems, with internally consistent, holistic outlooks, have become disturbed, or even fundamentally altered, in their outlook on nature because of the grafting on of new and alien ideas, or the over-emphasis on one minor aspect of their tradition in response to external pressure. For many individuals, there is a real tension between what they know in their heart is right, and the actual way their life is shaped and moulded by certain societal norms. What is happening to our beliefs which is pushing us to destroy or abuse the very things we say we believe to be important?

## "Western Materialism"

I want to start by looking at what have become the prevailing norms and belief structures for many in the West who do not see themselves as believers in any particular system. Such people are often less reflective about what they fundamentally hold to be true than those who express allegiance to a faith and have therefore to nail their colours to a particular mast. Secular thought shares many of the same roots as Christianity, but it has made some radical departures and developed new beliefs. Crudely speaking, we can call this secular thought "Western Materialism". With its roots in the growth of speculative thinking in the seventeenth century, it developed through the eighteenth century and has formed the background for many of the philosophical and socio-political movements which began in the nineteenth century. It is the underlying code for much which passes for scientific rationalism; for Marxism and for certain capitalist theories.

The basic beliefs of this materialist outlook derive from the Judaeo-Christian faith background of Europe. For instance, the belief in a linear progression of time is held by all but the most innovative of astronomers and cosmologists, along with a handful of reflective biologists. That idea of time has been used to validate a particular understanding of evolution, which has probably hindered our learning over the last hundred years, but which has appealed to our Western belief that we are top of the tree of life. Two evolutionary biologists, Eldredge and Tattersall, have described the way a Victorian value system took over the facts of evolution:

> *Some of the most mystic of scientific notions lie in the realm of evolutionary biology. Evolution—the proposition that all organisms are related—is as highly verified a thesis as can be found in science. . . . But HOW life has evolved is another matter entirely. Our standard expectation of evolution—slow, steady, gradual improvement, hence change, through time—is indeed a myth.*

> *Here is a scientific myth born of another myth more generally held by society at large in Victorian times: the myth of progress. The expectation that progress is inevitable paved the way for acceptance of a biological concept of evolution (which is good) and a specific notion of how that process works (which, it turns out, is not so good).*
>
> (*The Myths of Human Evolution*, Columbia University Press, New York, 1982)

The Victorians' experience of time and history was that things got better and better as year succeeded year. Progress was a fact, and its benefits were apparent. Thus the linear view of time, basic to the Judaeo-Christian tradition, which saw history as having a definite start (God) and a definite end (God), was re-interpreted to make a line stretching from first chemical explosion, through constant "improvement", to some great final End. Neither Judaism nor Christianity had been under any illusions about things or people getting better and better year by year. Sin, fear, anger, war, peace, hope, joy, were constants. As the Book of Ecclesiastes says:

> *What was will be again; what has been done will be done again; and there is nothing new under the sun.*
>
> (Ecclesiastes 1:9)

Only the circumstances changed, or were radically altered in their significance, as for Christians through the model of Jesus. But to secular Victorians, it was self-evident that life was progressing from the simplest to the most complex; from amoeba to homo sapiens; from the horse to the steam engine; from writing to printing; and from primitive tribes to the British Empire. This belief in progress fuelled the Empire and still fuels many aspects of Western materialism today. The belief in "progress" allows us to create nuclear waste with a life of 250,000 years, in the belief that "scientific progress" will eventually find a way of disposing of it!

Another Victorian secular idea which is still very prevalent is that of the survival of the fittest. This complements the Western idea of linear progress and development, of which the people of the West saw or see themselves as the highest expression. Naturally, such a theory appeals to those who feel themselves to have adapted most successfully: they are "the fittest". It also provided, and to some extent still does provide, a justification for the disappearance of other groups, including of human beings, who have not managed to keep up. Again, scientific data capable of a variety of interpretations was taken and used to "prove" just one. The theory of the survival of the fittest owes more to power relationships between Victorian social classes, and between the rulers of the Empire and their "primitive" subjects, than it does to rational, scientific exploration. The scientific data was hijacked, conceptually, and this hindered true research and development.

Western Materialism is, in fact, a sad distortion of what secular thought can be. Secular thought has produced a number of profound and important belief systems, such as internationalism. I want to look at these briefly to show how what I have outlined above is such a tragic distortion of secular thought. Later, we shall look at similar distortions of the noble creeds of Buddhism and Christianity. In all instances the proof of the pudding is the impact the belief systems have had on our environment and the extent to which they have the tools to respond positively or not to the ecological problems we face.

## Humanist internationalisation

Many of the best forms of secular Humanist thought involve belief in what is termed internationalism. This is the belief and hope that if humanity would forget its divisions or abandon its local and national expressions, then we could all work together for the betterment of our common world. In other words, we should think and act internationally, not just locally or nationally. This vision sees the great skills of humanity being pooled for the common good.

The roots of this belief (shared by secular belief systems such as Marxism and Humanism) lie in the two concepts we examined earlier—namely, the ideas of linear progress and of the survival of the fittest. However, internationalism takes these two concepts and places them within the framework of certain important goals, aiming at a greater good.

Let us start with the theory of the survival of the fittest.

This claims that evolution is the success of might or cunning over good. Survival is achieved by being bigger, quicker or more adaptable than other creatures. Human beings seem to bear witness, in their worst actions, to this theory. However, say the humanists, human beings are also capable of great compassion, self-sacrifice and distinct lack of concern for individual comfort, if others are in need. This is the raw material upon which internationalism is built.

Behind the humanist interpretation of the survival of the fittest is the theory of instinctive behaviour and humanity's development away from this. According to this theory, all species seek to survive and will instinctively use their powers to do so. A lion will hunt when it is hungry and does so instinctively. There is thus nothing moral or immoral about the behaviour of a lion hunting to kill for food. But humanity can decide whether or not to hunt. Humans can hunt for food, or for pleasure. They can also decide not to hunt but to preserve. Our capacity to make a moral choice and act accordingly is what distinguishes us from the rest of the animal world. It also underpins most of our perceptions about rights, enabling us to talk about human rights whilst we deny that such a concept of rights can or indeed should be extended to animals or other facets of the natural environment.

The humanists' belief in the development of the human capacity to choose, and to control base instincts, is just that—a belief. There is no way of proving or of disproving that at some point in our evolution we developed it. But the belief leads them to another, which—just as in the Judaeo-Christian tradition!—puts humanity at the top of the evolutionary tree and sets us apart from all other creatures.

Internationalists also understand linear progress in a very positive way. They see human history as a progressive movement from small, localized groupings, to tribal groupings; to small kingdoms; to larger states; to national states and empires; to federations of states; and ultimately, it is hoped, to a united world government. They believe that, because of evolution plus conscience, we are inevitably progressing to internationalism as our ultimate goal. This belief still fires many who hope for an end to separate states, be they capitalists wanting a free market in Europe, internationalists who want a pooling of human talents under one government, or international Marxists wanting an end to the class system under communism.

## Progress and determinism

These views combining evolution on a progress model with the belief in the arising of conscience in humans, fuel many people's ideas of reality and life. They are popular views, for they more than adequately provide the kind of mythic framework of meaning, place and role which Jung says we need. Ernst Fischer, writing about the impact of Marx's ideas combined with a simplistic understanding of Darwin in terms of inevitable progress, has this to say about the overall popular views which these two very different men gave rise to:

> *After Marx's death . . . his ideas . . . helped to form the world view of hundreds and thousands of people, acquiring, however, the accent of natural history which turned the desired development towards a socialist society into an 'iron Must of history'. . . . Not the least cause of this was the fact that Karl Kautsky, the principal popularizer of Marxism, had a background of Darwinism and, invoking certain passages of Marx, but especially Engels, imposed on the Marxist view of history a determinism deriving from natural history.*
>
> (*Marx in his own words*, Allen Lane, The Penguin Press, London, 1970)

The appeal of this simplistic amalgam of diverse views is that, because they sound scientific, they are more easily held as beliefs. For Marxists, there is very clearly a philosophy; for others, for whom Marx is not of significance, the appeal of social Darwinism and historical determinism lies in the apparent "objective" truth—with no need for higher, moral authorities such as God.

The effect which this de-deified concept of linear progress and the survival of the fittest has on our perceptions of nature should be obvious to all. It leads to a sense of ultimate authority to use the world. There are, however, two sides to that outcome. For many, that sense of authority has been used, subconsciously in most cases, as the excuse to exploit the world fully here and now. In the end, we have no-one other than humanity to whom we are responsible. If you extend the model of the survival of the fittest, then ultimately humanity breaks down into "us versus them", or "me versus you". It is a struggle model, not a cooperative one. However, the reverse is also true. If there is no-one other than humanity to whom humanity is responsible, then we have a corporate obligation to ensure that we carry out this responsibility for all those alive now and those to come. We have the world in trust. This is the genesis of most of the humanitarian movements of the world.

The secular humanist perspective is, of course, subjective, not objective. It views all things in relation to the key role of the human. However, secular humanism rarely articulates itself as a belief system, and so its values, beliefs, and norms are not normally placed openly on the table for all to see and debate over, as happens with belief systems such as Hinduism or Judaism which do state clearly that they are beliefs. There is a danger about this hidden nature of secular humanism's beliefs: it is not good when those who espouse this perspective pretend that they have somehow achieved a higher level of detachedness and truth, or fact, than those of other major philosophical belief systems. For it simply is not true.

## Science, values and culture

The extent to which Western science has been a vehicle for other rather disturbing cultural forces has been well-chronicled. But, gradually, science is coming to terms with the fact that what it discovers and then interprets raises questions of values, norms, ethics, morality, the nature of humanity and other equally vast and complex issues. Take, for instance, these statements from the Buddhist scientist Mahinda Palihawadana:

> *What is most obvious may be stated first: more than science itself, more than the inner nature of its methodology and its logic, it is the creeping materialism of new life-styles that has been cutting into both the visible cultural fabric and even the intangible spiritual content of the Buddhist religiousness.*
>
> *Anything that enlarges understanding is indeed desirable.*

> *From this and from its use of the principle of conditioned genesis [i.e.* karma-samsara*/wheel of reincarnation] in understanding things, it can be argued that the 'climate' that Buddhism creates is favourable to the scientific enterprise. But the scientific enlargement of understanding is welcome only IF it is conducted within the framework of the value system of Buddhism. While this may be inimical to science that is linked to power and violence, it does not at all affect the vast potentialities before science to aid in the total development of mankind.*
>
> ("Faith and Science in an Unjust World", *Papers from the World Council of Churches' Conference on Faith, Science and the Future,* WCC, Geneva, 1980)

It is important to stress here, with Professor Palihawadana, that science and investigation itself are to be welcomed. Too easily, "religious" people fall into a trap of dismissing science or the pursuit of learning about the natural forces of our world. To paraphrase Mao Tse Tung, it is not the pursuit we wish to destroy but the system which perverts it.

An example of the dangers within science, so uncritically accepted by the West, is spelt out in the disturbing book, *Fathering the Unthinkable,* by the scientist Brian Easlea. He argues powerfully that the military-industrial-scientific complex is fed by being essentially a masculine behaviour pattern operating in a world where men wage war against "feminine" values, women and "female" nature. It is the apparent success of this system, its seemingly endless ability to "deliver the goods", which Easlea sees as being so dangerous.

> *What, of course, makes masculine science particularly dangerous, as opposed to masculine prescientific magic and ritual, is that science truly 'works', that it really is efficacious, and therefore for the first time in history provides significant power over nature but provides it for men who are, to say the least, humanly ill-equipped to make wise use of that power.*
>
> (Brian Easlea, *Fathering the Unthinkable,* Pluto Press, London, 1982)

And the effects on the conservation movement of this unexamined coming together within Western culture of science and masculine, military, anti-feminine forces have been very serious, if not at points highly destructive. Let me illustrate what I mean.

In the world of the faiths, the central position often accorded to humanity is always tempered by the realization that humanity, like everything else, owes its existence to a higher power or powers. In the world of faith, the top position in the world carries with it a responsibility under God, the gods, or whatever you wish to term that which is the source of all being. In secular thought, as expressed by those who consciously describe themselves as humanistic, such a responsibility is still there, but is a purely human activity. This means that our sense of responsibility has to be constantly prodded in order that we act morally. However, few people who have adopted a Western Materialist outlook are as honest in their self-examination and adherence to basic values as avowed humanists. Thus responsibility becomes very narrow and economic. Ethics, as in the model of the faiths or humanism, are replaced by utilitarianism: essentially, an appeal to the selfish within everyone. The argument runs thus: if we don't care for the natural world, we could well find ourselves running short of those things which make life enjoyable. The reasons given for preserving or retaining anything in nature are solely in terms of whether it will be of possible use to us in the future. This is anthropocentrism taken to the nth degree. Read, for instance, the core philosophy of the World Conservation Strategy, drawn up in 1980:

1. *The aim of the World Conservation Strategy is to achieve the three main objectives of living resource conservation:*

   a. *to maintain essential ecological processes and life-support systems (such as soil regeneration and protection, the recycling of nutrients, and the cleansing of waters), on which human survival and development depend;*

   b. *to preserve genetic diversity (the range of genetic material found in the world's organisms), on which depend the functioning of many of the above processes and life-*

*support systems, the breeding programmes necessary for the protection and improvement of cultivated plants, domesticated animals and micro-organisms, as well as much scientific and medical advance, technical innovation, and the security of the many industries that use living resources;*

c. *to ensure the sustainable utilization of species and ecosystems (notably fish and other wildlife, forests and grazing lands), which support millions of rural communities as well as major industries.*

(*World Conservation Strategy*, published by IUCN-UNEP-WWF, 1980)

One understands the concerns which produced such a pompously anthropocentric document. But it is also disturbing how much of the myth of human "rights" over nature was taken uncritically into what is supposed to be a salvationary document for nature. In this document, nature is ONLY judged in relation to its usefulness to human beings. Nature has absolutely NO higher purpose or value than to be used by humans.

It seems to me that here we have a terrible irony. The humanitarianism of the conservation movement, drawing on the best in the secular humanist tradition, is now having to make common cause with the dark side of secular humanism in the form of anthropocentric, materialist utilitarianism. In doing so, conservation seems to be swallowing the seeds of its own destruction or rather the destruction of that which it aims to save. Let me spell out what I mean.

You can see how, in Western Materialism, utilitarian values have perverted the humanist belief that we human beings have evolved to a point at which we have developed moral responsibility and conscience. The belief in evolution and moral development has fallen prey to a desire for human self-aggrandisement, making humanity not only top of the evolutionary tree but also the centre of all meaning in the universe; nothing has meaning in its own right, except in relationship to human needs. The World Conservation Strategy's aims articulate this abuse of humanistic principles whilst still assuming an air of moral or ethical rectitude. The chain of argument which has led to the principles of humanism being reduced to utilitarianism is very simple. It runs roughly as follows.

The argument starts with a perfectly sound analysis, if a somewhat restricted one. The natural environment is being destroyed by people. These people can be roughly categorised into industrial concerns and national government concerns, and their over-riding interest is money. Therefore, we have to show them sound economic reasons for not wiping out the very resources they need in order to make money. If we can do this, then we can substitute controlled abuse for the headlong abuse which threatens to destroy major species and eco-systems for short-term gains.

We are, to put it bluntly, selling ecology. But are we selling ecology short? There is no doubt that, with certain already well-inclined groups, this approach pays dividends. But it is a very slippery road. For if you justify the continued existence of eco-systems and species on the basis of value to human life and economics, exactly who decides what is useful? And what does this mean for those aspects of nature which are currently deemed "not useful" or "not profitable"?

The most common example cited in support of this argument for environmental care is that of the armadillo. This South American creature is the only species other than humans to catch leprosy. In the last decade it has been discovered that, if you inject the footpad of the armadillo with a leprosy virus, it produces a serum which can then be used to help treat human sufferers of the disease. This has aided the treatment of leprosy in a very significant way. For this we should all rejoice. However, the argument of the economic conservationists is then continued: "Just imagine," they say, "if we had wiped out the armadillo BEFORE we knew it was so useful. We would never have been able to produce this serum, and countless thousands of humans would have continued to suffer." This is also fine as far as it goes. But let us just reflect a moment. Are we seriously proposing that the only purpose behind the evolution of the armadillo, over millions and millions of years, is that we can turn the poor creature upside down and inject its footpad with leprosy to help cure humans? What arrogance! What amazing self-centredness! Does the armadillo NEED human use to justify the evolutionary process which has created it? Is the only reason we can give for its continuing to be left alive one which places us as the teleological *raison d'être* for the armadillo's existence?*

The results of such thinking are an appalling slippery road to utilitarianism where, like Hitler, we are supposed to judge the value of everything living in terms of what we, in our very finite way, believe to be the purpose of existence. And the purpose of all existence is us. This is a frightening concept for anyone who either genuinely believes in evolution or genuinely believes in a Creator or Original Source, for it reduces all life to a meaningless mass unless given meaning by humans.

Not long ago, Heinz ran a wonderful series of adverts. Humorously, they asked: "Why has celery got a groove in it?" or "Why has a tomato got a dimple in it?" or "Why do lettuce leaves have a curl?". The answer was always so that you could pour on Heinz salad cream! A lovely picture of nature evolving over millions of years just to make life perfect for Heinz! They were joking: but the economic conservationists do not seem to be. They actually seem to believe that, by buying into the very value system which has laid waste much of our world, they can convert it. There is a famous adage about sending virgins into the brothel . . .

Nor are secular rationalism or Humanism the only systems to have produced such a distortion of their foundation beliefs. The dark side of human nature is able to pervert any system.

## Buddhism and its development in industrial Japan

The Buddhist teachings of compassion have always been taken to mean compassion for all creatures. Thus the taking of life for food has usually been seen by Buddhists as an evil from which

*By teleological I mean the End Purpose. For instance, in Islam, the teleological purpose of living according to the Will of God is that on the Day of Judgment you will go to Heaven, not Hell. Teleology is the final purpose for which developments in time are a means. Thus, the argument about the armadillo seems to say that some x million years of evolution of this strange but fascinating creature took place simply so that it could be of use to human beings.

people should be progressively weaned. Under Chinese Buddhist regulations, there are five stages of Buddhist discipleship. The most basic is that undertaken by the ordinary layman or woman who is supposed to refrain from eating meat on the first and fifteenth days of the lunar month. Next come those who forgo meat on those days and also on the major festival days of each lunar month; and then those who in ordinary life seek to avoid anything which contains meat. The fourth and fifth stages are two degrees of monastic life, where vegetarianism is compulsory. In Japan, under the influence of Buddhist teachings, a much stronger emphasis on vegetarianism developed, and by the Middle Ages Japan was an almost entirely vegetarian country.

The first precept—moral rule—in Buddhism is not to kill or harm any life, and this precept has exerted a profound influence on Buddhist communities. The Five Precepts—to abstain from killing, stealing, unlawful sex, lying, and the taking of intoxicants—are binding on all Buddhists. However, there have always been those who would happily backslide, and Chinese and Japanese stories abound with wayward monks who slip out for the odd bowl or so of meat, not to mention other earthly pleasures! Nonetheless, the principle of not causing harm has been constantly maintained, despite human weakness.

Japan has undergone many strange transformations since the disaster of her imperialism in the early half of the twentieth century, and her defeat at the end of the Second World War. We will examine some of these—namely, the rise of neo-religions based on ancient roots—later on in this chapter. But probably the greatest transformation has been that the Japanese have become the world's best industrialists and consumers. The frequent panics about Japanese "invasions" of the market spell this out only too clearly. Schooled by the USA, the Japanese have taken to heart the cause of industrialisation, consumerism and the free market.

This has called for some dramatic shifts in their lifestyles and, correspondingly, in their values. For a country which, a hundred years ago, ate virtually no meat now to be covered by hamburger and Kentucky Fried Chicken take-aways requires some shift of values. And that a country once renowned to foreign visitors as the place where animal life was respected should now be the chief criminal in aggressive excessive whaling, shows how even such fundamental beliefs can be altered.

It is not the function of this book to evaluate why or how this shift has come about—there is plenty of material on this. However, it is within our ambit to look at how a perversion of values has involved a perversion of religion and symbolism.

As mentioned above, Japan has a bad name second to none in the whaling community. Whilst other whaling nations have agreed, albeit grudgingly, to limit or even prohibit hunting of various species of whales, Japan has been the leading, aggressive advocate of a small group of recalcitrant nations. Yet this is a nation which, in centuries past, used to offer prayers for the souls of whales which had to be killed. It is a nation which traditionally has honoured the dolphin, but which now engages in one of the most appalling systematic slaughters of these beautiful and intelligent creatures. How is this possible?

A pathetic ritual is conducted regularly:

> *The Zen temple was large, opulently appointed and evidently prosperous. The occasion was a memorial rite to pray for the souls of the 15,000 who gave their lives in service to the Japanese people during the previous three years.*
>
> *The mourners were seated according to their rank in the company for which most of them worked. Twenty of them, male executives and government officials dressed in suits and ties, occupied benches on a raised platform close to the altar. The other 180 persons, mostly jacketless men but including a cluster of young women, sat crosslegged on straw mats to either side of the platform.*
>
> *Entering to the sounding of a gong, the priests filed in and faced the altar. A big drum sounded. One of the men in business suits stood and welcomed the congregation.*
>
> *The chief priest, wearing a canary-yellow robe and with his head shaved, began praying: "Release their souls from agony. Let them go over to the Other Side and become Buddhas." Then he and the other priests chanted, on and on, hypnotically, one of the sutras.*
>
> *When the chanting had ended, the mourners proceeded two-by-two to the altar to light sticks of incense.*

*Finally the chief priest delivered a short homily: "I am pleased that you have chosen our temple for this service. I used to eat whale meat in the army. And so I feel very close to whales."*

*The reference to whales wasn't at all out of place, since this service was attended by employees of Japan's largest whaling company. The 15,000 souls they prayed for were those of the whales they had killed.*

(Roshi Philip Kapleau, *A Buddhist Case for Vegetarianism*, Rider, 1983—from an article reprinted from the *Denver Post*, November 30th, 1979)

A ritual which was originally designed in the early period of Japan's conversion to Buddhism, to express the sense of value in other creatures' lives and to encapsulate the Buddhist virtue of compassion, has now become a ritual of exoneration of aggressive consumerism and utilitarianism. Not that this has gone unchallenged by other Buddhists—but the fact remains that Buddhism's symbolic expression of compassion has been manipulated to convey the reverse reality.

In this turning of the good to the bad lies part of the key to how we are taking concepts and symbols which once spelt life and wholeness and, by turning them inside out, are mentally shifting from life models to death model—a sort of suicide of the intellect. And there are other examples which seem to chart a similar distortion of the good to the bad, the growth or legitimisation of some kind of Freudian death wish.

## Christianity—the Calvinist interpretation

Christianity has often been blamed for the conceptual mess we have managed to create. As stated before, this is incorrect if one takes the true breadth of Christian witness—Orthodox, Catholic and Protestant. However, it is a justifiable allegation against certain perspectives in Western Protestantism, especially that branch of the faith which derives from the determinist views of Calvin. There is a story told of one of the more extreme Calvinist sects which arrived amongst the early settlers in America. They were quite brutal in their occupation of the lands belonging to both the native Americans and other settlers. Their justification was simply stated in their own "constitution":

1. *The Earth is the Lord's and the goodness therein.*
2. *We are the Lord's chosen ones.*
3. *The Earth belongs to us.*

In this arrogant story we see the corruption of the Christian message.

To understand what is happening, we need to look briefly at John Calvin and his teaching about the Elect. Calvin was part of what one might call the second wave of reformers. He lived from 1509 to 1564. Following the example of Luther and others, he rebelled against the Roman Catholic Church. In 1536 he took over the city of Geneva and made it a bastion not just of the Reformation, but of a particular development of Protestant thought which sought to come to terms with a basic question: How could the Lord of Justice (so essential when one engages in religious wars) be reconciled with the God of Love who "so loved the world that he sent his only begotten Son" to bear witness to that love? Calvin "solved" this by the concept of the Elect.

Calvin believed that certain people had been chosen by God—"elected" is the technical term—wholly without regard to their faith or actions. Rejecting the idea of universal salvation offered by God through the atonement of Jesus Christ, he taught that Christ's death and resurrection were meant only for the Elect. And how were the Elect chosen if not by their faith or works? Calvin brought to bear the doctrine of predestination. Before the Fall of Adam, even before Creation itself, God in his infinite and absolute wisdom had predestined certain of his people to salvation and the rest to eternal damnation. Thus, nothing anyone does will affect their fate. You may well ask, as have many Christians not of the Calvinist way, how you know you are one of the few Elect or of the many damned. Calvinism hedges on this, saying merely that those who fully accept Calvin's teachings are obviously the Elect as they alone are able to recognise the truth of which they are the extreme expression. It is what one might call a circular argument, just like the one used by the Calvinist settlers in America.

With this all-embracing theory, which not only deals with

the issue of a just, loving God, but also puts other "Christians" in their place, Calvinism launched an arrogant, self-centred perversion of Christianity. The model of the community of the faithful being like leaven in the loaf was transformed into a model of an inward-looking and self-satisfied Elect. The vision of the humble and the meek inheriting the Earth became that of those who humbled and subdued in order to take possession of the Earth. The stewards serving God in caring for his Creation became those licensed to exploit. And this they have done with terrifying consequences. A certain ruthless pragmatism, fused with religious certainty and inversion of the true meaning of the Gospel, has led to the usurpation of nature by the Elect, who historically have manifested themselves as founders and exploiters of "new" countries such as Australia, America and old Rhodesia (now Zimbabwe). Not all were overtly religious in the rather odd sense that the West uses that word, but they were, on the whole, shaped by the vision of the Elect and of the "rights" which such Election gave. Indeed, the men from Britain who carved up the old Imperial China, geographically as well as politically, spoke of Britain itself being elected by God to bring China to "civilization and Christianity". This was known as "manifest destiny".

The powerful consumerist effects of the Elect theory have not gone unnoticed. The idea that what I have and want I have and want by right is a very attractive one to many. The worst of the TV evangelists build their careers upon it. They equate success at work, having a bigger and better lifestyle, as sure signs of being blessed by God. The reverse of this philosophy—namely that those with little are cursed or ignored by God—is never stated, for it is in fact amongst the latter economic group that these mass media murderers of the Gospel find their strongest supporters.

The environmental impact of such an understanding of Christianity has been enormous. The Calvinists believed themselves to be in a superior position to all other people and peoples, and believed that they had a divine "right" to the world, and so they have acted with appalling contempt for other life-forms. Under the sway of the Elect have gone entire indigenous cultures, eco-systems and species. Nor have the other branches of Christianity been unaffected by the "success" of this brand of the faith. Other Protestant groups and certain sectors of the Roman Catholic Church have adopted elements of this perversion of Christianity. Witness the inability of the Church of England to come out with any clear teaching on ecology, or the failure of the Catholic Church to tackle the issues of population, development and conservation. There is still a feeling that anything which prevents "improvement" of one's lot, however understood, is some kind of unnecessary asceticism. These views now jostle for power with the older, more holistic approaches.

## The impact of the new "reality"

The reason for looking at these three aberrations in Humanism, Buddhism and Christianity has been to seek an answer to a fundamental question. What has caused the radical departure from the earlier norms of the faith to a position where the "right to use" has come to mean the "right to abuse"? I would contend that, in each case, those who have taken and turned upside down the myths and symbols, thought that they were responding "faithfully" to a newer reality—a more immediately satisfying and powerful reality—the reality of facts, money, human needs and wants being met. . . . The tragedy is that they were not only responding to, but also calling into being, this new "reality". And, like most monsters, it is now bigger than its creator and in danger of destroying all. This is what I now want to turn to. Having looked at the switchover from the use of nature, or relationships with nature, to the abuse of nature, I want us to look at how we, the children of the gods, made in the image of God, have sought to become, to play God.

## The image of the Apocalypse

Western activism in areas such as the peace movement, development aid and conservation is primarily, but usually subconsciously, driven by belief in and fear of the Apocalypse. The term is used with such gay abandon that it might be helpful to pause and look at what the Apocalypse is.

Judaism and Christianity, along with Islam and modern

science, posit a linear view of time, existence and history. The creation had a specific starting point and will thus have a specific end point. As mentioned in Chapter 1, for Jews this is seen as the Coming of the Messiah and the resulting Judgment Day. For Christians it is the return of the Son of Man (Jesus) and the coming of the Kingdom of God, with the Judgment Day as precursor to that Kingdom. In Islam, it is the combination of the Days of Resurrection and Judgment, the prelude to which is the Dreadful Day—the Day of Wrath. In all three traditions there is a fearful vision of this Dreadful Time. It is perhaps best known in the words and images brought together by John, the writer of the Book of Revelation, the last book of the New Testament:

*The seven angels that had the seven trumpets now made ready to sound them. The first blew his trumpet and, with that, hail and fire, mixed with blood, were dropped on the earth; a third of the earth was burnt up, and a third of all trees, and every blade of grass was burnt. The second angel blew his trumpet, and it was as though a great mountain, all on fire, had been dropped into the sea: a third of the sea turned into blood, a third of all the living things in the sea were killed, and a third of all ships were destroyed. The third angel blew his trumpet, and a huge star fell from the sky, burning like a ball of fire, and it fell on a third of all rivers and springs; this was the star called Wormwood, and a third of all water turned to bitter wormwood, so that many people died from drinking it. The fourth angel blew his trumpet, and a third of the sun and a third of the moon and a third of the stars were blasted, so that the light went out of a third of them and for a third of the day there was no illumination, and the same with the night.*

*In my vision, I heard an eagle, calling aloud as it flew overhead, "Trouble, trouble, trouble, for all the people on earth at the sound of the other three trumpets which the three angels are going to blow".*

*Then the fifth angel blew his trumpet, and I saw a star that had fallen from the heaven on to the earth, and he was given the key to the shaft leading down to the Abyss. When he unlocked the shaft of the Abyss, smoke poured up out of the Abyss like the smoke from a huge furnace so that the sun and the sky were darkened by it, and out of the smoke dropped locusts which were given the powers that scorpions have on the earth: they were forbidden to harm any fields or crops or trees and told only to attack any men who were without God's seal on their foreheads. They were not to kill them, but to give them pain for five months, and the pain was to be the pain of a scorpion's sting. When this happens, men will long for death and not find it anywhere; they will want to die and death will evade them.*

*To look at, these locusts were like horses armoured for battle; they had things that looked like gold crowns on their heads, and faces that seemed human, and hair like women's hair, and teeth like lions' teeth. They had body-armour like iron breastplates, and the noise of their wings sounded like a great charge of horses and chariots into battle. Their tails were like scorpions', with stings, and it was with them that they were able to injure people for five months. As their leader they had their emperor, the angel of the Abyss, whose name in Hebrew is Abaddon, or Apollyon in Greek.*

*This was the first of the troubles; there are still two more to come.*

(Revelation, 8:6–9:12)

*Then I heard a voice from the sanctuary shouting to the seven angels, "Go, and empty the seven bowls of God's anger over the earth".*

*The first angel went and emptied his bowl over the earth; at once, on all the people who had been branded with the mark of the beast and had worshipped its statue, there came disgusting and virulent sores.*

*The second angel emptied his bowl over the sea, and it turned to blood, like the blood of a corpse, and every living creature in the sea died.*

*The third angel emptied his bowl into the rivers and water-springs and they turned into blood. Then I heard the angel of water say, "You are the holy He-Is-and-He-Was, the Just One, and this is a just punishment: they spilt the blood of the saints and the prophets, and blood is what you have given them to drink; it is what they deserve." And I heard the altar itself say,*

*"Truly, Lord God Almighty, the punishments you give are true and just."*

*The fourth angel emptied his bowl over the sun and it was made to scorch people with its flames; but though people were scorched by the fierce heat of it, they cursed the name of God who had power to cause such plagues, and they would not repent and praise him.*

*The fifth angel emptied his bowl over the throne of the beast and its whole empire was plunged into darkness. Men were biting their tongues for pain, but instead of repenting for what they had done, they cursed the God of heaven because of their pains and sores.*

*The sixth angel emptied his bowl over the great river Euphrates; all the water dried up so that a way was made for the kings of the East to come in. Then from the jaws of dragon and beast and false prophet I saw three foul spirits come; they looked like frogs and in fact were demon spirits, able to work miracles, going out to all the kings of the world to call them together for the war of the Great Day of God the Almighty.—This is how it will be: I shall come like a thief. Happy is the man who has stayed awake and not taken off his clothes so that he does not go out naked and expose his shame.—They called the kings together at the place called, in Hebrew, Armageddon.*

*The seventh angel emptied his bowl into the air, and a voice shouted from the sanctuary, "The end has come". Then there were flashes of lightning and peals of thunder and the most violent earthquake that anyone has ever seen since there have been men on the earth. The Great City was split into three parts and the cities of the world collapsed; Babylon the Great was not forgotten: God made her drink the full winecup of his anger. Every island vanished and the mountains disappeared; and hail, with great hailstones weighing a talent each, fell from the sky on the people. They cursed God for sending a plague of hail; it was the most terrible plague.*

(Revelation, 16:1–21)

This powerful language has fed the imaginations of the people of Europe for over a thousand years. As the end of the first Christian millenium approached—the year 1000 AD—popular imagination, priestly moralists and rulers began to expect the literal fulfilment of the prophecies. In his excellent study *The Pursuit of the Millenium*, Norman Cohen has shown how, throughout European history, at moments of social, economic and religious tension, the vision of the Apocalypse has been evoked and various groups have seen themselves to have been chosen to help implement this event. The language and imagery have even passed into the secular form via Marxism, where they exert just as powerful a pull, only this time it is the Communist Movement, or Historical Inevitability, which takes the place of both God and the Chosen Ones. Hence the emphasis on the Party having to lead all decisions, and its right to use terror tactics to bring the end of the old regime, as in Stalin's thought or the mad horrors of Pol Pot in Cambodia.

On an even wider plane, as indicated before, this imagery has fuelled, mostly subconsciously but also consciously, humanitarian concerns such as the peace movement or conservation. It has given people both a sense of being special—part of a purpose greater than themselves—and a true sense of the gravity of the threat to which they are responding. That few within these groups can recognise the religious roots of this apocalyptic vision is irrelevant. It is there, and it works. One who understands the power of the apocalyptic language is the nuclear disarmament writer, historian and activist, E. P. Thomson:

> *The paradox is this. In times of disturbance in the past our ancestors were often seized with apocalyptic visions. We now inhabit daily a civilization which is, for the first time, technically equipped to enact the apocalypse: the opening of the heavens, the cremation of infants, the rivers of blood.*
>
> (E. P. Thomson, *Writings by Candlelight*, Merlin Press, 1980)

Whilst, in many instances, fear of the Apocalypse has led to activities of an important, humanitarian nature, sadly this is not the only response that apocalyptic imagery has brought forth. I wish to illustrate how this fear is being used or handled in various faiths, ideologies and "movements", and the extent to which the moral and ethical climate it creates generates a mixture of utilitarian hedonism, quiet despair, and very short-term vision, expectation and planning. All of this, of course, affects the way we then perceive and use the natural world—a world which, according to the apocalyptic tradition, is to be destroyed in order that a new world, a better creation, might arise.

The key problem in all this use of such powerful, religious imagery is that of God! In the older religious understanding of the Apocalypse all the destruction was wrought by God—the Beginning and End of Creation, the Alpha and Omega. Thus it could be seen as purposeful, as having some meaning because God as Creator can indeed bring about a new creation.

> *Then I saw a new heaven and a new earth; the first heaven and the first earth had disappeared now, and there was no longer any sea. I saw the holy city, and the new Jerusalem, coming down from God out of heaven, as beautiful as a bride all dressed for her husband. Then I heard a loud voice call from the throne, "You see this city? Here God lives among men. He will make his home among them; they shall be his people, and he will be their God; his name is God-with-them. He will wipe away all tears from their eyes; there will be no more death, and no more mourning or sadness. The world of the past has gone."*
>
> *Then the One sitting on the throne spoke: "Now I am making the whole of creation new," he said. "Write this: that what I am saying is sure and will come true." And then he said, "It is already done. I am the Alpha and the Omega, the Beginning and the End. I will give water from the well of life free to anybody who is thirsty; it is the rightful inheritance of the one who proves victorious; and I will be his God and he a son to me."*
>
> (Revelation, 21:1–7)

But now it is humanity which is in danger of destroying life on this planet. And yet we do not have the morality or creative powers of God. Before going into this more deeply, let's look at some rather startling examples. They are cited not as condemnations, but as parts of what seems to be a general pattern; they seem to point to a growing sense of cosmological insecurity—a lack of any true understanding of meaning and purpose in life.

## Sikh militancy

In the Punjab it has long been the case that the Sikhs have lived side by side with their Hindu, Muslim and occasional Christian neighbours.

Sikhism originates with the teachings of Guru Nanak (1469–1539 CE). Guru Nanak was born into a Hindu family, in the area of northern India dominated by the Muslim Mogul Empire. In his teachings he sought to find the truth which lay between what he saw as the over-zealous Muslims and the variety of sects of Hinduism. He stressed the oneness of God and the importance of service to all people. After him came nine other Gurus, many of whom were persecuted by the other religions for their teachings of love, service and opposition to religious hypocrisy. Many of the teachings, prayers and poems of these Gurus were gathered together in the Sikh Holy Book, originally known as the *Adi Granth*. Also included are prayers and poems of Hindu and Muslim holy men.

By the time of the last human Guru, Guru Gobind Singh (1666–1708), the Sikhs were suffering terrible persecution. This forced the Guru to form a brotherhood, known as the *Khalsa*, to defend the Sikh community against violence. But in the true spirit of Sikhism the *Khalsa* could only take up arms to defend the faith, the poor, widows and the young, regardless of whether such people were Sikhs or not. When Guru Gobind Singh died, he named the *Adi Granth* as the final Guru, thus ending the line of human Gurus. To this day, the Holy Book, now known as the *Guru Granth Sahib*, shapes the lives of the Sikh community with their deep belief in the oneness of God, the creator of all, and the unity of all peoples. Sikhs are renowned for their hospitality—they provide a free kitchen at their temples for all in need; for their teaching of equality, in particular the equality of men and women; and for their sturdy defence of the helpless, no matter of which caste, creed or colour.

Their reputation for integrity has always stood them well. Yet in recent years the picture has radically changed. The demands for a separate Sikh state—Khalistan—have led certain sectors to take up arms in an attempt violently to create such a state and drive the non-Sikhs, especially the Hindus, out of the Punjab. The siege of the Golden Temple of Amritsar in 1985 marked a watershed in this movement as many formerly concerned Sikhs, seeing their holiest shrine violated, turned from debate to violence.

In the midst of the social and political upheaval a new trend has emerged within certain factions of Sikhism—a sense of an impending cătastrophe which ranks with classic descriptions of the Apocalypse. Previously, the Sikhs have vigorously maintained the non-divine nature of their Gurus—they are seen as wise men through whom God speaks. But in recent years, the last human Guru, Guru Gobind Singh, has begun to be elevated, if not to a human/divine status, then at least to a quasi-Messianic role. With this has come a set of teachings, revolving around the Guru, and which reflect this shift and paint in fairly graphic terms what the impending event is to be. The teachings, known as the Ninety-Nine Prophecies of Guru Gobind Singh, purport to be prophecies which the Guru made about the development of the Sikh faith after his death. And if you read those up to about prophecy 97, they do appear to faithfully "foretell" the key events of Sikh history up to 1985. After that, the prophecies become very dramatic, envisaging an all-out war between the Sikhs and India, culminating in total devastation out of which God then calls the Sikhs to statehood. It is unclear what happens to the rest of India, let alone the world. But what is clear is that certain sections of Sikhism—a reincarnational, cyclical faith—have responded to the general state of anxiety and to the power of elitist concepts of status (i.e. the "right" of Sikhs to have their own state and to rule over others) by flattening the cyclical into a linear view, and have thus prepared the ground for the growth of a militant millenarianism. They expect that, by their actions, they can force the new age to begin, much as Christian extremists hoped to force the hand of time and bring Christ to rule for 1000 years. This thousand years is the origin of the term "millenarianism".

## Messianic Christians

The growth of fundamentalist Christianity and its links to apocalyptic attitudes and expectations have been well chronicled by, amongst others, the Christic Institute in Washington and the novelist Gore Vidal. Christian expectations of the millenium are as old as the faith itself, but in Orthodox, Catholic Christianity, they have usually manifested themselves as passive—an awaiting of the Second Coming, as in St Paul's fervent prayer when in the midst of persecution: "Come, Lord Jesus, come—Maranatha." However, since the early Middle Ages, there has also been a tendency in Western Christianity to try to "force the Hand of God", so to speak. This has taken both benign and destructive forms. A wonderful example of a benign attempt is shown by the American historian Barbara Tuchman in her book *The Bible and the Sword* (Papermac, 1982).

Lord Shaftesbury was one of the nineteenth century's greatest philanthropists and social reformers. Throughout his life he struggled against child labour, industrial exploitation, poor housing and so on. His energy and concern were fuelled by his strong evangelical Christian beliefs. Yet he always felt that the true resolution of the world's woes ultimately lay outside of this world. He naturally sought to do all that he could do here and now, but it was the hope of a "new heaven and a new earth" where "there would be no more death, and no more mourning or sadness" which really inspired him. For he shared the majority vision of the Christian faith, that if only humanity would try to move towards a community based on love and justice, then Christ would appear to bring this to fulfilment.

To this end, Shaftesbury studied his Bible to see what was necessary to help the Lord of Life return, for then all the cruelty against which the reformer struggled would be swept away. He found that central to the Bible's teaching about the conditions necessary for the Second Coming was that the Jews in the Holy Land should come to accept Jesus as the Messiah. Lord Shaftesbury pondered on this and on the failure, to date, of the Church to convert the Jews. He concluded that the attempt had failed because the faith had been presented only by the Roman Catholic Church. Lord Shaftesbury was convinced that, if the "non-superstitious" teachings and simple rituals of the Church of England could be presented to the Jews of the Holy Land, then they would convert, the stage would be set for the return of the Messiah, and so the hated world of oppression and cruelty, poverty and greed would be forever vanquished. In this belief, Shaftesbury was one of the prime movers for the establishment of the Anglican Diocese and Cathedral of St George's, Jerusalem, and indeed contributed much of the necessary funds. That his hopes were not realised, nor perhaps could be realised, should not prevent us from admiring the deeper humanitarian concerns which expressed themselves in the bricks and mortar of the oh, so English Cathedral in Jerusalem.

An example of a destructive attempt to "force the hand of God" was the "Kingdom of God" incident in Munster. In 1534, Protestant extremists took over the city of Munster and declared that they were preparing the way for the Messiah. In order to hasten his coming, they killed their opponents, both Catholics and moderate Protestants, and established a Kingdom of God which was to foreshadow the Kingdom of the World which Christ was soon to inaugurate. As the religious leaders' idea of the Kingdom seemed to consist mostly of dictatorship and sexual licence for themselves, it is not surprising that it was soon overthrown in a bloody uprising and attack by other Protestants and Catholics, uniquely linked by their distaste for the extremists.

Benign and destructive models of action, inspired by the Apocalypse, jostled along side by side for many centuries—a case of saints and sinners. But now a shift in thinking, or in the putting into practice of the thinking, has come about. Now we have the technological means and arrogance to believe that *we* can enact the Apocalypse, the "melting of flesh", the "rivers of blood", the destruction of vast populations. And we have the pride to do so. Suddenly our environment, our world, is expendable, by us. And so, fuelled by the belief that they are the Elect, certain groups are willing to try to bring about the Battle of Armageddon, when the Anti-Christ is finally brought to account by the Messiah. They see the possibility of World War III as the fulfilment of the vision of St John, as the harbinger of the Second Coming. The development of horrendous nuclear arsenals and of biological weapons and the destruction of the natural environment are all signs for them that the End is at hand, and if they can speed up the situation, then the Apocalypse will come sooner. To this end, they are willing to promote international tension and to encourage the arms race, convinced that the Anti-Christ is the USSR and that the forces of good are represented by the USA.

The main authority on this view has been Hal Lindsey who, in his massive bestseller *The Late Great Planet Earth*, interprets the "fire on Magog", described by the prophet Ezekiel, as a prediction that nuclear missiles will annihilate the Soviet Union. Jerry Falwell, founder of the USA Moral Majority and one of the more famous TV evangelists, has come to similar conclusions. "The Bible predicts a Soviet invasion of the Middle East", he told the *Los Angeles Times* in 1981. "And it is at that time when I believe there will be some nuclear holocaust on this earth . . . and Russia will be the offender and will be ultimately totally destroyed."

The approach of such apocalyptic thinking was summed up and condemned by religious leaders of all the major churches in the USA in a statement made in 1985. Their description of the fundamentalist Christian viewpoint captures the core of that apocalyptic vision:

> *In recent years a movement known as the Religious Right has become a significant force in American politics. . . . Through these leaders, a religious doctrine—the ideology of nuclear Armageddon—has entered our nation's political arena. This doctrine seems to justify nuclear war as a divine instrument to punish the wicked and complete God's plan for history. According to Armageddon ideology, the social crises and nuclear war dangers of our time are signals that history is entering its final stage: an era of extreme violence and nuclear warfare beginning in the Middle East and ending with the destruction of God's enemies in the Battle of Armageddon. In the Armageddon worldview, this final era is foretold in Holy Scripture, constitutes God's plan for humanity and cannot be prevented. The ideology of nuclear Armageddon identifies our nation's enemies with the enemies of God.*
> (Christic Institute Religious Leaders Declaration, Washington D.C., 1985)

Apocalyptic, evangelical fundamentalist thinking has also manifested itself in two ways in Reagan's government. Firstly, he has on a number of occasions wondered aloud if this is the last generation! Secondly, his former Secretary for the Environment, James Watt, believed that Jesus would come again in the first decade of the twenty-first century. Therefore he saw no reason to protect the natural environment because everything would bc destroyed and built anew in twenty years' time anyway. Thus he was quite happy to permit mining and deforestation programmes in the national parks. Luckily he was ousted within two years of appointment.

## Japanese messianism

Finally, let us look briefly at how those in some of the new religions of Japan have responded to the fear of the End of Time. Again, a situation of radical change, supposedly contained by abiding traditional values, has left many Japanese disorientated. Out of this situation a vast array of new religions have arisen. They are usually based on Buddhism, but focus on charismatic leaders who develop their own teachings. Here again the concept of the Elect is powerful and the literature of these groups abounds with phrases such as "the seed people of the Holy 21st century" or "Spiritual teachers of the coming Unity of Mankind". Such grandiose phrases and ideas offer a vision of a central importance for the believer and a hope that the world as it exists now will be changed. Indeed, a belief in the termination of the current world is crucial to many of the new religions. All of them have a similar formula: the world is heading towards total destruction. This can only be stopped by people turning to the Truth. We have the Truth and when everyone recognises this, we can usher in a new time of earthly paradise.

Sometimes there is some hope about the future in the apocalyptic vision, even if it is still rather unlikely. In a number of sects there is a belief in a vast continent, called Mu, which is supposed to have been the birthplace of all civilisation. This continent of Mu grew corrupt and was destroyed, leaving only the islands of Japan as evidence of its former existence. The decay of morals which began in the last years of Mu has continued to this day and the final great upheaval and punishment will be the Baptism of Fire and the Storm of Raruro. This "now threatens to destroy the human race. Only if the Five Colored Races are reunited under the Japanese Emperor and the teachings of the Sacred Phoenix, Okada Kotama, is there any hope for mankind." (Winston Davis, *Dojo—Magic and Exorcism in Modern Japan*, Stanford University Press, 1980)

The unusual thing about these quasi-Buddhistic Japanese faiths is that they have lost the cyclical view of most traditional religious thinking in Japan, shaped by Buddhism and Shintoism. There has always been a belief that this present cycle would end and that the ending would come about because the world had grown corrupt and evil. But because the "soul" survives and all life is filled with these souls, the end would never be the final end but the end of one cycle only. All would be reborn and recreated again. However, in the new religion, it is as if the cycle has been flattened, so as to create a linear approach to the end of this world and to leave in the air the question of any recreation or reincarnation. And again, the evidence of environmental destruction and the fear of nuclear warfare have fuelled the teachings of these groups and the formation of their visions of the future.

## The motivation for conservation

These three examples of the modern developments of different faiths show how very diverse belief structures have responded to certain widespread fears within our world. In all cases, the mainstream faiths see the developments as aberrations, and yet these have grown with great speed and show little sign of flagging. Their importance to us and our relationships with nature is that they are fundamentally responses to the same forces of fear which motivate the peace movements and the conservation movements. Both of these, as I have said, are apocalyptically-influenced movements. Their fundamental motivation comes from a genuine fear that we could indeed be the last generation, or amongst the very last. Their literature is full of dire predictions of environmental collapse if we continue to treat the world as we are currently doing. Yet, ironically, the very same fear of the Apocalypse lies also at the root of our exploitative attitudes. If the world is going to end, let's make the most of it now and go hang the future—if there is to be any future. The question therefore arises: Can one of the major causes of the crisis also provide the means of the salvation?

Recent surveys of children's attitudes to the future have proved one disturbing thing. Most Western children fear that the world may be destroyed during their lifetime. This leads to two basic responses. One: "If the world is going to end, I may as well get the best from it while I can"—what one might call gentle hedonism. Two: "This world is too important to let it be destroyed. What can I/we do to prevent this happening?"—the roots of activism. Report after report on children as young as six or seven show that these two responses are fundamental to the way in which they construct their world view. Whichever one they adopt then shapes their expectations of themselves and of the future.

It seems to me that, in Western society, you can see these two responses lived out in everyday life. The peace movements and the environmental movements are part of the second response. The titles of many of the more dramatic reports capture both the apocalyptic thinking and the sense of a "religious" mission—for instance, the World Wildlife Fund's *How to save the world* or the USA Carter Government's report *Global 2000*. In this sense we can see both how the movements are tapping into powerful symbols within their own cultures and how they are determined by the cultures from which they have grown. There is no peace movement worthy of the name in India or in China, nor is the conservation movement in either place motivated by the same sense of urgency, except with regard to certain key species which carry other symbolic messages, such as the tiger or the panda. Quite simply, the apocalyptic mentality is linked much more to a linear view of time than it is to a cyclical view. Appeals to action based upon apocalyptic fear will hardly be comprehended in cultures where time is viewed as cyclical.

This came across very clearly recently when I and my colleagues from the International Consultancy on Religion, Education and Culture were with the BBC filming in a North London school. We were discussing with 13–15 year-olds their views of the future. The school was very multi-cultural, and this was reflected in the group. The Western-originating children all responded along the lines of the two basic responses outlined earlier. They were very obviously affected by a fear of the End. But the Hindu children were not worried. They spoke quite easily about how Lord Shiva ends each world cycle by fire and yes, perhaps this might be in the form of nuclear destruction this time, but so what?

To return to the conservationists motivated, albeit unwittingly, by apocalyptic fears. Because of the current avowedly secular, materialist stance of conservation, it is digging its own conceptual grave. It uses as a foundational perception the apocalyptic model. Yet it leaves out the Divine, because that does not fit with its mythology of science. Conservationists seem to be wanting to have their conceptual cake twice over. They wish to draw on the undoubted powers (good and bad) of the vision of the End (apocalyptic and otherwise) of the Judaeo-Christian tradition. They then try to find the means of salvation by using another model of mythology and belief—namely what is often referred to as scientism.* By positing that humanity is top of the evolutionary tree, but that there is no higher or ultimate power for this top position to be in relation to, conservation is operating on a self-destruct model of reality. It is motivated by fear that we humans, indisputably now managing the world, will destroy the means of life and thus enact our own Apocalypse. Yet its only source of hope for this not taking place is these self-same humans being motivated by good will. By toppling the Divine from the model of reality, we leave ourselves as both object and subject, as both the problem and the solution. Yet we are continuing to use a model of the End which predicates a belief in a power greater than us and in a moral purpose to history. By continuing to use a model which assumes salvation—"How to save the world . . ." – we are left with having to believe that we can be our own salvation.

The effect of this is very simple. Many people using this secular model of linear belief and motivated by the general fear

*Scientism is the name given to the use of pieces of scientific information in order to create a supposedly "objective understanding of life". This usually incorporates ideas such as evolution = progress and survival of the fittest.

of the Apocalypse have simply no hope that things will change. They see the task of conservation as being to keep things going for as long as is possible before the inevitable happens. Thus they look for answers and alternatives to current crises within the very system which has created the problems in the first place and find to their surprise that there are no answers, no new ideas or attitudes. The secular myth of the omnipotence of humanity and the human intellect's ability to solve all problems has led us into a blind alley, because those very concepts prevent us from making a new assessment of reality—a new set of values. We seem to be conceptually incapable of breaking free of the very constraints which shape us. We have turned our backs on the force which was always seen as the source of hope, transformation and salvation within that model—namely the Divine—and we are not bold enough to explore other conceptual models which might help us to break the hold of this way of thinking.

This is the final irony of our making ourselves into gods. We have become our own jailers, not our own saviours. The anthropocentric view, devoid of the Divine but operating on an apocalyptic model, ultimately condemns us to death because no higher or greater purpose can be given to counter our innate greed and destructiveness. The very model of reality which is currently used to underpin conservation is, in fact, our primary problem. The question then arises: how can new perceptions and new conceptual models be found which will enable the energies attracted by the conservation and peace movements to discover new ways of really transforming the world? If we are not to sink into either the hopelessness of gentle hedonism, or the Elect theories of the three distortions of traditional faiths, as outlined above, we must explore alternative, workable models of reality, which can offer new ways of viewing and treating the environment.

# 3

# Other Eyes—Other Worlds

The intention of this chapter is to see how the world appears through diverse lenses formed by different belief systems. In this exploration, I have taken certain phenomena of the natural world, and looked at how various faiths understand these and relate to them. Let me stress right away that I am not interested in suggesting that everyone become a Taoist *feng shui* master, an aboriginal initiate or an Orthodox monk! This is not what the chapter is about. What I do hope is that, through realising that each phenomenon can be perceived from radically different perspectives, we can find insights which can inform and help shape the world in which we each believe. In each culture's model of the world there are blank areas, misconceptions, things which simply do not make sense. It is in recognising this, but also appreciating the positive elements of our own traditions, that we can come to see what other traditions can offer to us—and we to them. Without such a cross-fertilisation, our current world models seem incapable of offering sufficient insight and flexibility to lead us through the environmental chaos which we have created.

## How faiths grow

Throughout history, faiths and cultures have interacted, and from this interaction have arisen the particulars of each faith, which divide one from another, as well as the beliefs or values which unite them. In the past, this interaction took place at a much slower pace and usually through the channels of traders and scholars, myth-tellers and story-makers. The passage of time has made the insights that various faiths in fact share seem as though they were specific to just one faith or culture, the exclusive discovery or revelation vouchsafed to that faith alone. But the study of the history of religion shows a much more dynamic interaction. I would urge upon us today this model of interaction, and of each faith finding something distinctive to share and possibly to gain from recognising how big the pool is within which we are all swimming. But at the same time as we grapple with our apparent belief that we are the only fish in the pond, it is also right that we should seek to remain faithful to our own traditions. Many people fear that, by acknowledging "truths" within other traditions or ways of life, they will weaken or corrupt their own beliefs. But this is sadly to misunderstand the nature of religion. The following examples illustrate the spirit in which I hope readers will view the insights offered later on from the different faiths.

## From Buddha via Islam to Tolstoy

Leo Tolstoy, the great nineteenth-century Russian novelist and Christian, underwent a conversion experience which radically altered his life. One factor in his conversion, and in the conversion or religious life of many thousands of other Russian Christians, was the story of Saint Barlaam and Saint Josaphat. The main theme of the story concerns a young and wealthy prince called Josaphat who meets an otherworldly monk or hermit called Barlaam. The example of this man of God leads Josaphat to be baptised a Christian, to leave his throne and kingdom and to go into the wilderness to lead a life of Christian contemplation and asceticism.

This simple but moving story brought many to an appreciation of Christian truths and a new kind of lifestyle. But the fascinating thing is where this Russian tale came from. A hint lies in the story. The prince is pictured as an Indian prince who is converted by a Sinai desert monk, Barlaam. The Russians got the story from the Greek Orthodox Church, who also passed on a version in Latin to the Western Church, reaching Iceland, for instance, in an Icelandic translation in 1204 CE.

The Greeks got the story from the Georgians—Central Asian

people who were among the first to become Christians. They got it from the Muslims! The story was virtually the same, except that conversion led to Islam rather than Christianity. The Muslims got the story from that earlier Central Asian faith, the Manichaeans. And the Manichaeans? Well, they got the story from the Buddhists! For this is the story of Siddhartha Gautama, who left all his wealth to become a wandering ascetic after seeing four sights which challenged him to reflect upon the true meaning of life—sickness, old age, death and a monk.

So this story has functioned as a vehicle of faith, as a means of conversion, as a purveyor of meaning, within four major faiths. And the question remains: Where within this story lies the truth which is particular to just one faith?

## Feminising God and the Buddha

Another example of the interaction of faiths in the development of specific faith identities is how the feminine has entered into masculine faiths. The ancient Egyptian religion was a very male-dominated, judgmental faith, in which the chief characters were the great male gods of the sun, the moon and the afterworld, whilst here on earth the Pharaoh ruled as the male principle. Great indeed was the indignation when females came too publicly into the realm of the throne. Yet the feminine side of divinity cannot be excluded and, in Egypt, the cult of Isis, the faithful but also determined and resourceful wife of the God-King Osiris, grew to enormous but often unofficial status. The basic model of Isis showed her holding her son Horus, whom she raised to avenge her husband's death. So powerful was this combination of faithful wife, loving mother and active womanhood that it became dominant not only in Egypt but throughout the later Roman Empire—where the faith structure was equally male-dominated.

Almost certainly, the basic imagery and inspiration of the Virgin Mary and Christ come from the cult of Isis with her son Horus. Again, here is a faith dominated by the masculine and yet out of it grows a profound belief in the divine capacities of the female. One only has to look at some of the eleventh- and twelfth-century Virgins to see that this is not just a saintly woman. This is God the Female. There is little doubt that, in many minds, the Virgin is equal to the Father in divinity, and certainly in approachability and efficacy.

The link between Isis and the Virgin is well-known and well-chronicled. There is also a less well-known link between the Virgin and the Bodhisattva Kuan Yin, in Chinese Buddhism. In its imagery, Buddhism is as aggressively masculine as Christianity and, again, the feminine is allowed into Buddhism in a slightly unorthodox way. It is primarily in China and Japan that this occurs, and the female figure is known in Chinese as Sung-tzu Kuan Yin—Kuan Yin, the bringer of children. Kuan Yin begins to appear in the eighth to ninth centuries and emerges from the Persian end of the Chinese Empire, near the beginning of the Silk Road. This was an area where, as Marco Polo reported some four hundred years later, Buddhists and Christians dwelt together, for many of the border Turkish tribes had become Christians of the Nestorian persuasion. The remainder of the tribes were heavily influenced by Tibetan Buddhism in its Tantric form.

Within Tantric Buddhism, the figure of Avalokitesvara—the Lord of compassionate glances, or the Lord who looks down—has always been popular. He is the bodhisattva of compassion par excellence; and the model of saving compassion which he established formed the model for much within the development of the bodhisattva idea. A bodhisattva is one who has followed the Buddha's teachings and, over many rebirths, has reached a stage of total enlightenment. From this stage the bodhisattva—which means "enlightened being"—could enter nirvana and extinction of being. But the bodhisattvas' compassion for the rest of humanity and indeed for all sentient life is such that they delay their entry into nirvana in order to save as many beings as possible. This they can do because of the vast store of merit which they have built up over their many lives. If anyone genuinely calls upon them for help, they will assist that being to a better rebirth through the influence of their merit.

Avalokitesvara is male in the Tibetan tradition. By the time transformation has taken place, he appears in popular Chinese belief (worshipped by both Taoists and Buddhists alike) as the female Kuan Yin, the Goddess of Mercy and the child bringer.

Indeed, outside modern Chinese hospitals in mainland China, you can sometimes find large, officially funded statues of Kuan Yin, who has always been believed to help with pregnancy and other female ailments. But what happened to turn the male bodhisattva, Avalokitesvara, into the female Goddess of Mercy, the bodhisattva Kuan Yin? How did the all-male hierarchy of the Buddha and the bodhisattvas become in the popular Chinese imagination a hierarchy of the Buddha and the saviour Bodhisattva Kuan Yin with all other bodhisattvas, divinities and spirits subject to her? The key seems to lie in the extraordinary cross-fertilisation between Christianity and Buddhism that took place in the areas of Central Asia, along the Silk Routes, where ancient Graeco-Indian cultures, Nestorian Christians and Buddhist civilisations dwelt side by side for centuries. Here the feminine in religion, now expressed by the Virgin Mary, met the male, the Buddha, and a new expression of the feminine—Kuan Yin—emerged.

As in the previous example, we have a common theme—the power of the feminine—diversely interpreted, yet always fulfilling basically the same emotional and religious needs. And again, the question of which interpretation is "right" and whether, therefore, there is any "wrong" one simply does not arise. It is in this spirit that religious growth and development have always taken place. To be sure, it then becomes necessary at certain points for the official leaders to define that which is particular to their tradition, but unless the faith is dying anyway, such definitions do not freeze the religion, for to do so is to kill it. They simply act as a recognition of past trends and set certain limits on the future direction.

For instance, the first four centuries of the Christian faith saw many controversies, and Councils which sought to deal with these by defining Christian belief, so that by the end of the fifth century the key elements of what constituted Christianity had been delineated. It was from that point on that the faith was able adequately to move into outreach amongst the tribes on the borders of the Roman Empire and, in doing so, absorbed quite happily all manner of older rituals, festivals and even gods, who reappeared as saints. And, in the process of defining what Christianity was to be, the Church Fathers of the first five to six centuries used Hebrew thought, Greek philosophy, Roman pragmatism, aspects of the mystery cults including Isis, and found no great difficulty in working in Latin, Persian, Indian, Syrian, Armenian, etc, as the Christian faith spread amongst the cultures of the Middle East, Asia and Europe.

So, interaction between cultures and faiths is nothing new. It is the very foundation of faith itself. Nor is this limited just to the intellectual level. Art, as in the example of Isis/Virgin Mary/ Kuan Yin, also plays a crucial role in helping believers conceive of their world. Because it does not rely on words, art passes with greater ease, at times, between cultures and enables people to—quite literally—see things in a different way.

In the last chapter we looked at negative interactions between belief systems, in many cases arising from the fear of extinction—the very fear which motivates so many in their concern for peace and ecology. Now we need to turn to the vast resources which the belief systems of our world hold in trust for us, to see if there are different ways in which we can view that which we think we know and understand. For it is fairly obvious that our current models of thinking are not working—at least, not if we wish to pass on to our children a world which is worth living in.

## The Land

How do we view the land? Well, it's sort of there, isn't it? But how do we talk about it and what do we understand it to be? Often when I ask these questions, I get completely blank looks! What is the poor fellow raving on about now? Land is land, isn't it? Well, is it?

## Talking of land

In the West, the language used to describe land falls into two main categories. The first kind of language we use stems from the monastic system of farming which was pioneered by the Benedictines and in places fused with the older Celtic Christian traditions. Within the Celtic Church many earlier "pagan" ideas were carried forward, including an innate sense of the sacredness of nature which was to flow as a sub-theme in Western Christianity until it was made respectable by St Francis in the twelfth century and then sentimentalized by the later Church.

The Benedictines, established in the sixth century, managed to work the land efficiently, without continuing the vast ecological destruction which the Roman Empire had caused. The later stages of the Roman Empire, with its centralized structure of food distribution and land use, the growth of vast private estates, and the feuding Emperors all needing power bases and massive armies, wrought more ecological damage on North Africa, Egypt, Asia and Western Europe than any other single force until the Industrial Revolution. The creation of the Sahara desert by the over-farming of the formerly fertile fields of North Africa is well-known. The Benedictines preserved in their farming the efficiency which had been introduced by the Romans, but this was shaped by their sense that they did so as stewards of the Creator God. Their attitude towards the land therefore fused well with the concept of the sacredness of the land, which was apparently inherent in the peasantry's view but which had lost its influence when the local farmers had been forced off the land by the massive estates of the late Roman Empire.

Remnants of the farming patterns established by the Benedictines are still to be found in traditional farming language. The land is spoken of as being a living force. Thus, following the Biblical ruling on letting the land lie fallow for one year in every seven, the land is said to be "resting". The land has to be "fed", "tended", and it "brings forth" its harvest, like a woman giving birth. Indeed, the language used to describe the land, and the caring attitudes towards it, often has feminine associations. The land is seen as having meaning and purpose, albeit in association with human needs; but, nevertheless, it also has meaning in its own right. Land is that which simply exists, in one sense; it is the "given" of existence, but given by God, and therefore purposeful.

The second kind of language we use about the land arises from a newer attitude towards it. The land is not viewed in any sense as having a life or meaning of its own; it exists through the meaning which we give it. In this language the terms used about land are "undeveloped", "ready for exploitation", "unused". The land is seen in economic terms only and its significance is purely in terms of how we can use it. In this world, the land is "sprayed" and not fed, and that which dwells upon it which we do not want is "controlled" by chemical forces. In this world, a natural forest is a wasted forest. A "real" forest is serried ranks of pines designed not to provide a habitat, nor even to look pleasant to the human eye, but to be "economically viable".

It is this language, which sees the land as having no value unless it is used by and for us, which has enabled us to tear out hedgerows because they "waste" land. Try telling that to the birds who have nowhere to build their nests, or to the top soil which has no barriers to its wind-blown travels. It is the language of a system which views streams and rivers purely as means of irrigation and not as features of a natural landscape. So we turn the wandering streams and rivers into straight, canalised irrigation channels, and gone are the banks for voles or water-rats, or the slow-flowing pools for the variety of river plants. Listen one day to the language of those who have destroyed much of Britain's countryside, and in the very images they use you will hear the death knell of the land as a natural environment. And, again, it is so often the economic argument which is put forward, in favour of new ways, despite the many examples and experiments which show that, using traditional methods of land use and fertilisation, the crop yields will be as high and the costs in chemicals lower.

Occasionally the two languages and models of perception clash and it is not without significance that one language will talk of the "rape of the land", while the other speaks of unexploited land as "virgin".

But how do other cultures view the land, and what can we learn from them which might help save us by re-orientating our concept of it?

## Feng shui

One of the most fascinating and most usable ways of seeing the land is the very ancient Chinese science of *feng shui*. This is geomancy, or, to use the rather prejudicial English term, earth magic. But, to the Chinese, such a term is not relevant. "*Feng shui*" literally means "wind water" and this is an indication of their fundamental view of the world, and especially the land, as being full of life.

As we saw in the first chapter, Chinese traditional belief sees the world, and indeed all beings, as maintained by the interaction of two forces, *yin* and *yang*. *Yin* and *yang* are within everything, even within what Westerners would see as "inert" land. Indeed, it is in the land that these forces are most powerfully at work, as regards everyday human existence. For the Chinese, the land is not inert, nor without meaning until we give it meaning. For them, even the older Western tradition does not go far enough. In the beliefs of *feng shui*, the land is literally alive with forces which have shaped the earth and which continue to dwell powerfully within it. The land is occupied long before any human being sets foot on it, and human participation in the landscape has to be in terms of a recognition of these existing forces and a willingness to work alongside them or even under them. The difference from the Western model should be obvious. This is a partnership between land and humanity, the like of which is unknown in Western thought.

## Superstition or wisdom

It is interesting to look at how Westerners have reacted to this science before we consider it in detail. The following quotes show clearly how the system of *feng shui* is a challenge to Western values. In his study of Chinese religion, *The Dragon, Image and Demon*, the Revd Hampden C. DuBose wrote in 1886:

> . . . . *it* [feng shui] *retards progress, forbids railways, closes coal mines, prevents enterprise, checks new efforts at advancement, interrupts the free thought of the people, and keeps them wrapped in the mummy folds of ancient prejudices.*
>
> (*The Dragon, Image and Demon*, published by Partridge and Co, London)

In 1873, in his book *Feng-shui*, the Revd E. J. Eitel wrote about the reverence for nature which he found in the system:

> *I say would to God that our own men of science had preserved in their observatories, laboratories and lecture rooms that same child-like reverence for the living powers of nature, that sacred awe and trembling fear of the mysteries of the unseen, that firm belief in the reality of the invisible world, and its constant intercommunication with the seen and the temporal. . . .*
>
> (*Feng-shui*, first published in 1873, reprinted 1973 by Cokaygne, Cambridge)

## Of dragons and tigers

In basic *feng shui* thought, the landscape is a reflection of the forces which dwell in it. A hill or mountain is described as a dragon, whilst the valley is seen as a white tiger. The terms are used to highlight the sense of great powers and forces inherent in the land. Some Chinese may believe literally in dragons and white tigers; but for many these are images, indicating the forces at work. However, the imagery is useful, for it helps to explain graphically some of the very complex practices and theories of *feng shui*. For example, in planning buildings, no-one in his or her right mind would dream of building on a dragon's head, for fear of waking him. In a land often struck by violent earthquakes, the sense of riding a dragon or a tiger can be very real. Furthermore, no-one would dream of building in such a way as to dominate the dragon's height, for this would be to usurp the authority of the dragon. Thus Chinese sensitivity to natural skylines has been considerable; whilst pagodas and other elegant, spire-like constructions have been built as being in harmony with the skyline, hills and mountains have not been dominated by vast blocks of buildings.

The considerations of *feng shui* do not stop at the monumental level. They also affect what height your ordinary house should be—basically, in scale with your environment—and what steps you should take to restore the balance of forces which you have inevitably disturbed by your building. This can be done primarily through the planting of trees and bushes or by the creation of gardens. The overall effect is to create a landscape which remains within the scale of the environment and seeks to reflect and enhance the main natural features, colours and fauna of the area rather than destroy them. Water is thought to play an important part in such a landscape, as are auspicious directions. *Feng shui*'s attention to those details is echoed in our recent discoveries that people are actually far more content when near expanses of water or rivers and streams, and that the physical direction of a home, office or even room and bed can affect us physically as well as "spiritually". Likewise, the Chinese have known for centuries, if not millenia, what we have only recently learnt the hard way, through the disasters of high-rise buildings: that scale is of vital importance to our well-being and sense of one-ness with our environment.

The key to *feng shui* is the Master—a man trained in sensitivity to the natural and constructed environment. The main tool of the Master is his compass, and the very complexity of this captures the feeling of being a part of something bigger and greater than mere humanity. The compass can have up to thirty-six rings on it, each relating to a different factor which has to be taken into account when divining an area. Whilst this can lead to an at times apparently endless process of decision-making, it does instil a basic respect for the land and a sense that not just your own immediate wishes have to be taken into account. Thus, on the thirty-six-ring compass (the correct title for this compass is the *loupan*), the first two are connected with the Eight Trigrams, semi-magical configurations which relate to the eight directions and are associated with the *I Ching*. The third ring locates the dragon on the site; the fourth is for the testing of the waters; the fifth gives you the stars of the dragon, which tell you whether it is a benevolent or inauspicious one. The seventh uses the mariner's compass points to help determine the best sites for the burial of the dead.

*Feng shui* has two major roles in Chinese life. The first, which we have already started to look at, is to determine the position of places for the living to dwell in. However, it is arguable that the second role of *feng shui*, to site the burial place of the dead, is the more important. Because of the belief in the role of the ancestors in the continuing well-being of the family, it is vitally important where you bury your dead. To bury an ancestor in an inauspicious grave, where the earth factors are not good, is to hang a ghostly albatross around your family's neck. For the unhappy, ill-at-ease deceased will take revenge upon the family by causing death, illness, misfortune and natural disasters. Knowing where to bury the dead is vital.

The rings continue outwards, covering such topics as the Ten Stems and Twelve Earthly Branches of the Chinese horoscope system; the twenty-four stars of divination; the sixty pairs of stems and branches for fortune; the special stars for determining the sand of the area; various systems for determining which forces are present that are auspicious for burial; the spheres of influence of good and bad forces within the land; the Five Elements and their roles in the area (the Five Elements are Wood, Earth, Fire, Metal and Water); the correct correlation of certain stars with the siting of cities; the twenty-eight constellations which bring certain attributes to the areas they guard; the twelve gods who determine when it is a good time to move into a new house, make a major alteration or bury the dead; and so on. All this is in addition to the basic feel of the place, and the rules about height and general environment in terms of flora, which I mentioned earlier.

The result has been that, on the whole, Chinese architecture and design have sought to flow with the forces inherent in a given landscape, rather than trying to dominate them or simply ignoring them. The Chinese use of land has been marked by the feeling that, whatever humanity does, it is only a part of the whole. We can flow with the whole, or we can work against it. If we flow with, then all will be well: we shall be at ease in our environment. If we flow against, then for a while all may seem to be well, but eventually disaster will strike. Modern-day *feng shui* experts point to the very short honeymoon period we have had in the West with high-rise blocks, and say that this is a classic example of exactly why *feng shui* is a science to be taken seriously.

## Revolution to re-evaluation

It is of interest to note the changing attitudes within China itself. In the early years of the modern Communist state (from 1949 onwards), *feng shui* was either ignored or, as in the period of the Cultural Revolution, persecuted and ridiculed. In this period, when it sought to mimic the West's Industrial Revolution, China produced classic examples of terrible planning and building, coupled with gross industrial pollution and destruction of the natural environment. Now that these chickens are coming home to roost, in terms of disease, vandalism, discontent and inner-city problems, the government has turned back to *feng shui* to provide help in planning. It has been able to do this, in the same way as it has also turned for help towards traditional Chinese medicine—namely, by finding scientific evidence which makes the traditional system look serious. Yet it is obvious that what is most important to the modern Chinese government is not just that the old system seems to prevent our worst excesses, but that it actually bespeaks an attitude to the land and to the natural world which is necessary if we are literally to "feel at home" in our own world.

An interesting example of this shift in official attitudes by China has involved one of my Chinese colleagues in the International Consultancy on Religion, Education and Culture (ICOREC). Kwok Man Ho is a fully-trained *Feng Shui* Master. He has performed countless *feng shui* services for the Chinese community throughout the UK. Recently, the Chinese government has been looking at the possibilities of opening a vast Chinatown in the London Docklands scheme. The idea was to build a replica of a Ching dynasty (seventeenth–eighteenth century) town. Before the site was seriously considered, our colleague, Man Ho, was invited by the Chinese government and local Chinese entrepreneurs to inspect the site and say whether the *feng shui* was good or not. His report recommended that extra waterways be cut, nearly twice as many trees be planted, the heights of some of the buildings be lowered, and certain sites set aside for temples or shrines to the earth gods and Kuan Yin. All this was then incorporated into the plans. Would that other developers, including my own beloved government, were open to such modifications!

## The power of naming

Now this may have sounded all very interesting, but what can *feng shui* offer to the sceptical Westerner? How can it "work" for us? The answer lies, to some extent, in the power of naming. One of the things which is so powerful about *feng shui* is that it names areas, according to the perceived forces within them. Thus that which might otherwise have remained implicit is made explicit. In our own culture, naming has lost most of its power. The names for many of our places are in old languages, and so it is no longer immediately obvious what they mean. There are few people, for instance, who, travelling through Salford, realise that it means "the ford by the willows"! The habit of naming new areas after the local councillor who was in power on the appropriate committee at the time has been of little help in giving a sense of belonging to the local environment. The council estate I grew up in, on the outskirts of Bristol, was called Hartcliffe, after a quarry some fifteen miles away. It meant nothing as far as the local area was concerned, as there were no cliffs and not a great many harts! We also had a clinic named after a Councillor. The Councillor was Mrs Nutt. The clinic was soon called the Nut House . . . but that's another story!

Yet rediscovery of the physical phenomena which gave rise to a name can be very important. Take, for instance, Bristol. The name means "the bridge over the river". Now, for centuries, Bristol was beautifully dominated by its marvellous twin rivers and their docks. Ships sailed into the heart of the city, and the church towers responded to the soaring masts, to give a famous forest-like effect. Then the ships changed and grew too big for the river Avon. The city's reaction, until very recently, was to cover over the now redundant river space. The heart of Bristol was taken out—the bridge over the river almost ceased to have any meaning. However, in the last decade, the waters have been rediscovered. The city centre is again alive with ships and masts, and the old docks are buzzing with waterfront activities from boating to art galleries and cafés. By rediscovering its waters and turning to face them again, the city of the bridge over the river has regained its heart.

But often we need actually to find new names for our area, so dead have the old ones become. Many people grow up in places which they feel have been shaped by forces that they cannot change. They become fatalistic—such and such a place has always been like this. A few years ago I ran a multi-faith education centre in Salford, concerned with the inner city. In our work with children in Greater Manchester, we often met groups from areas with quite literally bad names. One game we played was to get the children to rename their home area by looking at it through *feng shui* eyes. So, children who had always felt that "this is how things are" suddenly found that their estate was "the place of the dragon's paws", or of the "head of the white tiger". They began to be aware of the natural phenomena which the planners have so often done so much to hide or destroy. By seeing the streams and rivers as living snakes which bring life to the area, they could appreciate that the burying of these streams and rivers into culverts has actually taken away from the natural sense of the place. They could see that the scale of buildings should be in proportion to the scale of the environment; that flat areas need clumps of trees to break the flow of the white tiger, who otherwise will devour all in his path and turn the flatness into barrenness. Through renaming, through making the familiar unfamiliar and new, children (and, it has to be said, teachers!) became aware of the actual components of their home area and began to see that imaginative use of these could really enhance it. This is all in the tradition of classic *feng shui*, which calls forth those forces which are already in the land, so that we can make ourselves at home with them and be accepted by them. If you like, it is all a question of scale.

In recent years, much of the practical wisdom of the *feng shui* system has come to be acknowledged by architects and planners in the West. We seem to find it relatively easy to take certain insights and ideas from something as old and established as Chinese culture. I now want to look at another set of values concerning the land to which we have not taken with anything like the ease with which we have accepted the Chinese ideas, even though it comes from an even older culture.

## Australian aboriginals

Part of the problem for us in the West is that, before we can really come to appreciate other perceptions, we have to deal with two issues. Firstly, as we have explored above, we need to recognise the shortcomings and, at times, actual inconsistencies of our own perceptions and traditions. Then we have to deal with the fact that we have many misconceptions about other cultures and that these have effectively innoculated us from viewing them as in any sense our equals. This, after all, has been a necessary part of our cultural, religious and ideological imperialism. So, before we can approach certain traditions, we have to undo years of conditioning which have led us to denigrate some, if not, in fact, virtually all, other cultures. The problem is that when we realise what we have done in the past, our attitude then swings like a pendulum and we end up with a glorified, romantic view of the other culture(s) which is almost as bad as the former imperialistic view, for it still does not allow the people to be themselves, but only a vehicle for our own sense of identity. Amongst the peoples to whom this has happened are the Australian aborigines.

The image portrayed of the aborigine has generally been that of a human being who is barely human. Aborigines have been literally hunted like wild animals—as in the deliberate policy of the British in Tasmania to kill all aborigines there, a policy which was concluded in 1870 with the death of the last one. They have been dispossessed of their land, had their women attacked, their children taken away, and their traditions destroyed. The way in which the aborigines were perceived by most people is evident from this extract from a Religious Tract Society publication of 1841, which suggested, remarkably, that there could be a different view:

> *We have often heard these poor savages upbraided with their treachery, their dishonesty, their cruelty; with their sloth, and ignorance of the distinctions between right and wrong; yet we have acted towards them, as if they were in every respect enlightened in the practices of civilized nations; as if they, who are under a law unto themselves, were under obligation to ours, and understood them too; we have made little allowance for the*

*influence of principles diametrically opposed to our own, and which have originated a system of conduct in them which we have no right to condemn, under existing circumstances.*

*(The Visitor or Monthly Instructor for 1841*, London)

It is an old strategy. If you wish to dispossess people, first take away their rights to be treated as fellow human beings. This was and is still done to the aboriginals, and it has made it very difficult for Westerners to hear what the aborigines have to say in the realm of values and beliefs. Yet, in aboriginal thought, there is one of the most powerful and potentially exciting visions and understandings of the natural world that the world has to offer.

## The Dreaming

The core of aboriginal belief is expressed in the idea of the Dreaming. Before the Dreaming began, the land was flat and lifeless. Then came the Dreaming; a time when, from the earth itself, or from the waters or the sky, ancestral beings emerged and journeyed across the landscape. These ancestral beings were the ancestors not just of particular tribes of human beings, but also of particular animals. This therefore gives a very intimate relationship between certain peoples and certain creatures. On top of this, each person will have one particular animal which is special to him or her. This will depend on where the person was conceived and on the Dreaming ancestor who is associated with that place.

Central to the aboriginal world view is the song or story map of the land, which relates the physical features of the landscape to the wanderings and adventures of the Dreaming. As the Dreaming ancestors travelled, they often fought, hunted, made love or engaged in dances and magic. The results of these actions are the mountains, valleys, outcrops, earth colouration, waterfalls and so on which give the land its features. Perhaps the most difficult for non-aboriginals to grasp has been the idea that the very pathways which the ancestors walked are sacred and meaningful to the aboriginal. Thus, what looks to us like featureless flat land will be full of story meaning to an aboriginal. Nor is this story or song knowledge just old tales for the fireside. It is quite simply a matter of life and death—both for the individual who is wandering in that landscape and also for the whole of life.

The telling of stories is the very heart of aboriginal life and culture, for the stories have a power which is far greater than the story-teller, or the practical information which they contain. The story-telling rites are very secret and only the initiated are told the stories in any detail. A man or woman who knows the full story-line of a particular ancestor is given great respect and authority. The first reason for this is that the stories help make survival possible. The story-lines, which turn what seems to be desert into a map of its vital sites, a sort of story or song map, contain vital information for survival in the tough and, at times, downright inhospitable environment of the bush. If you know that that slight depression over there was made by the honey-ant ancestor, then that tells you that that is where you will find some honey-ants to give you food. Likewise, if you know that a Dreaming ancestor made water, or brought water forth, at a certain spot, you can walk with confidence from one such place to another, knowing that you can find water. Someone travelling along the Gammon Ranges, to the area of Lake Frome and Lake Callabonna, will know that the Dreaming ancestor snake Arkaroo travelled that way, drinking both lakes dry and carving out the Arkaroola gorge with his over-heavy body full of water. But he will also know that Arkaroo stopped at various places along the way and that these can be recognised by the physical signs which are left of the giant snake's resting. Furthermore, he will know that in these places he will find water, even if he has to dig down for it.

Whilst the pragmatic usefulness of the stories and songs is obvious, even to the outsider, they also have a much more important function. This is that they keep the world alive. Without them, life would depart and the world would relapse into emptiness and meaninglessness. The importance of the story is that it keeps singing the world into being. When the Dreaming ancestors departed, they taught their descendants, both human and animal, how to live. This is how the distinctive lifestyles and behaviour patterns of the various peoples and creatures evolved. Part of the teaching given to humans was how to perform dances and rituals which would keep alive the spirit of the land and the waters. These rituals, and the stories which accompany them, are the literal lifeblood of creation. Only by their constant telling and retelling can the Dreaming continue. For Dreaming is not an event in the past—and here we return to the different concepts of time which we looked at in Chapter 1. Dreaming, and the ancestors themselves, are not things which happened in the past, as we understand this in our linear way of thinking. They are events which happen, or are happening – and the present tense here should be understood to contain both the past and the future too.

Quite simply, English grammatical rules are such that it is impossible adequately to express in our language the very different idea of time held by the aborigines. I will try to put it another way, for the idea is crucial to our understanding of the power of the aboriginal view of the land. Telling the Dreaming stories makes the events happen again. Time is related not to a sequence of events, but to a place. To be in a place which has a Dreaming story, and to know or to tell that story, is to be responsible for that story having happened and for all the physical effects to which the story relates. Time becomes compressed into one time—being. It is only through the constant telling and reliving of the stories that life is sustained, for such telling and reliving make the stories "happen". Dreaming is something of which the people are part, and yet the Dreaming would die without the people.

What this does to the concept of land is dramatic. First of all, the land is full of meaning and purpose. Secondly, you, as the story-teller, as the descendant of the Dreaming ancestor, are responsible for it. But there is absolutely no sense that the land is owned by the people. Rather, the land owns the people, and either one without the other would die. Thirdly, the life force which links the land, the creatures and the humans is sustained on behalf of all life by the story-telling and rituals of the human descendants of the Dreaming ancestors. Fourthly, those ancestors are there, physically and spiritually present in the land, and they live through the telling of the stories and through the correct behaviour and care of the human beings.

It is the fact of the Dreaming being a present happening which has caused such violent clashes, over mining, for instance, between the aborigines and white culture, which cannot conceive of such a sense of beingness nor of the sacredness which arises from it. What white developers have seen as waste land is, to the aboriginals, full of Dreaming significance and Dreaming ancestors and, therefore, full of sacred power. To dig into it without being aware of the life forces contained in the land and its features is inconceivable to aboriginals. So, when white settlers have bulldozed water-holes or sacred trees, have tunnelled through ranges, or placed railways across sacred pathways, these actions have been as traumatic to aboriginals as if a force alien to us decided to demolish a city school and hospital with all the children and patients, teachers and nurses still inside, in order to make way for a tennis court! There are countless well-attested stories of aboriginals, hundreds of miles away from their most sacred site, suddenly falling ill and even dying because someone has destroyed that site—unaware of its inherent life force. To aboriginals, every act of destruction is a diminution of the very forces of life itself.

This understanding of land and life is perhaps most easily understood by non-aboriginals in relation to the arguments over uranium mining. The desire to mine uranium—so essential to all nuclear processes—has led white developers into areas considered sacred by the aboriginals. The aboriginals have tried to defend these sacred areas which legend has specifically stressed should never be disturbed, for to do so will cause untold destruction and suffering. In this case, they have found some assistance from non-aboriginals who also—though for different reasons—see the taking of uranium as contributing to the threat of destruction of our world through both "peaceful" and "military" development of nuclear forces.

## Being the land

The sense of being owned by and responsible to the land does not mean that nothing can ever happen. What it does mean is that care has to be taken and the life forces present have to be taken account of and respected. This is wonderfully captured in

Bruce Chatwin's book, *The Songlines*, in which he recounts the slow but steady progress of the laying of a new railway line across central Australia. The officials in charge are working with the aboriginals in ensuring that no sacred sites are damaged or threatened, and so the line will have to follow the lie of the land much more than if it were being planned by ordinary Western rules. The feeling of being responsible to the land and its forces comes across very forcefully. In this excerpt Chatwin is talking to the non-aboriginal man who works with the aboriginals on siting the new line:

> *'In theory, at least, the whole of Australia could be read as a musical score. There was hardly a rock or creek in the country that could not or had not been sung. One should perhaps visualise the Songlines as a spaghetti of Iliads and Odysseys, writhing this way and that, in which every "episode" was readable in terms of geology.'*
>
> *'By episode', I asked, 'you mean "sacred site"?'*
>
> *'I do.'*
>
> *'The kind of site you're surveying for the railways?'*
>
> *'Put it this way,' he said. 'Anywhere in the bush you can point to some feature of the landscape and ask the Aboriginal with you, "What's the story there?" or "Who's that?" The chances are he'll answer "Kangaroo" or "Budgerigar" or "Jew Lizard", depending on which Ancestor walked that way.'*
>
> *'And the distance between two such sites can be measured as a stretch of song?'*
>
> *'That', said Arkady, 'is the cause of all my troubles with the railway people.'*
>
> *It is one thing to persuade a surveyor that a heap of boulders were the eggs of the Rainbow Snake, or a lump of reddish sandstone was the liver of a speared kangaroo. It is something else to convince him that a featureless stretch of gravel was the musical equivalent of Beethoven's Opus 111.*
>
> *By singing the world into existence, he said, the Ancestors had been poets in the original sense of the poesis, meaning 'crea-*

*tion'. No Aboriginal could conceive that the created world was in any way imperfect. His religious life had a single aim: to keep the land the way it was and should be. He trod in the footprints of his Ancestor. He sang the Ancestor's stanzas without changing a word or note—and so recreated the Creation.*

(Bruce Chatwin, *The Songlines*, Jonathan Cape, London, 1987)

New phenomena can also be sung or have stories told about them. The Dreaming, precisely because it is, in our sense, timeless, can grow. Therefore, a new feature on the landscape, which is sensitively aware of the older features, can have its own story or song, since all creation, all life, is contained within the land, and it is the power of the story or song to constantly bring it forth or to bring it forth for the first time. Aboriginal thought is not static, but it is framed by the sense of being owned by and responsible to the land and its life. This is well captured in this poem:

*We belong to the ground*
*It is our power and we must stay*
*Close to it or maybe*
*We will get lost.*

(Narritjin Maymuru, Yirrkala, quoted in *Australian Dreaming—40,000 Years of Aboriginal History*, edited by Jennifer Isaacs, Lansdowne Press, Sydney, 1980)

## Dreaming our own dreams

Again, to the question, "How nice but so what?" I can only refer to the experience we have had at the Salford centre and since then in religious environmental work, using this approach with children and teachers. We ask groups to invent their own Dreaming stories or songs related to specific physical phenomena which they know. We ask children (and teachers) to choose certain natural features in a given area—it can be as small as the school grounds or as large as the whole estate or district. They then have to "name" these features by telling a story about their formation. For instance, a depression in the

school playing fields—what made that and why? A sharp bend in the river; a straight line of trees; a small incline—what story can be made up to "explain" each of these? Naming is obviously an important aspect of this, but so is the sense of belonging in a continuum of time. "Dreaming" means you see yourself in relation to things which had a life long before you, are now in time with you, and will outlive you. This activity is also important because it gives a chance to explore the idea of being owned by the land, and this so radically challenges our normal outlook on life that we in the West have to turn many other values upside down.

In all three world views (or four, if you count the Western traditions we have looked at as two) what you believe the land to be and what you believe to be your "rights" to the land have a fundamental effect not only on the way you view the land but also on how you actually use it. The differences between the world views are very real and substantial. Each view has its problems, for all traditions have a tendency to fossilise; actions or attitudes become a matter of habit rather than expressing a living awareness of the richness and creativity of the tradition. Yet within all the world views there are insights which can be shared between cultures, and this is especially important when a culture comes to appreciate that it has lost an ability to relate creatively to the land.

Let us now turn to another natural phenomenon and see what understandings we can glean from diverse traditions about trees.

## The trees

### Acts of God—folly of humanity

In recent years the trees of the United Kingdom, particularly in the southern half of England, have taken a severe battering. First there was Dutch elm disease, which virtually wiped out those beautiful trees and left gaunt skeletons in the fields, hedgerows and on the tops of hills. Then came the hurricane of October 1987, which wrought destruction on the parks, commons and forests of the south, leaving many fine and ancient

trees stretched out like so many fallen after some horrendous battle of the Titans.

The effect of these two attacks on the treescape of England has been to make some people aware of how much they had taken for granted with regard to trees. Because of their size and slow rate of growth, trees appear just to "be"—a "given" element of the environment. Yet we have been losing and transforming our tree cover over decades and centuries, and what we have left now is but a fraction of what existed five hundred years ago. Over the last one hundred years we have failed to plant new trees to keep pace with the natural loss, and so older trees have been left more exposed than nature would allow and thus more vulnerable to the full force of the winds. This is part of the reason why so many older, taller trees were destroyed in the 1987 hurricane. Again, what many would like to call "an act of God" is, in fact, as much an act of humanity.

But another assault on our trees has attracted far less attention, presumably because it is not, literally speaking, in our own back gardens. This has been the destruction of natural woods and their replacement with conifers. The serried ranks of conifers marching across the hill country of Scotland, Wales and Dartmoor have largely been ignored. However, the impact on our woods of purely economic forces (conifers grow quicker and straighter than indigenous trees) has been to effect a change far greater than that caused by Dutch elm disease or the hurricane. For the planting of the forests of conifers has meant not only the diminution of the number of our indigenous trees but also the loss of the natural habitat which these trees provide for other species.

## The killing of the forests

Compared with what is happening world-wide, the situation in the UK is nothing. In the last few decades, various factors have combined to threaten not only many of the ancient forests of Europe, but also the formerly massive tropical forests of the world.

The sheer pace of destruction of the rain forests in the last thirty years is mind-boggling. Every minute, rain forest cover

equivalent to over twenty football pitches is cut down or consumed. Every year, between 11 and 15 million hectares of tropical forest are destroyed—an area larger than Scotland. The catalogue of what has already gone is appalling:

*The Philippines—55% forest loss between 1960–85;*
*Thailand—45% forest loss between 1961–85;*
*India—all primary rain forest destroyed;*
*Bangladesh—all primary rain forest destroyed;*
*Sri Lanka—almost all primary rain forest destroyed;*
*Haiti—all primary rain forest destroyed;*
*China—50% loss of forest in S. Province of Xishuangbana;*
*World-wide—over 40% of all tropical forests destroyed.*

(Details from WWF International)

Meanwhile, in Europe, acid rain caused by industrial pollution in the air has led to the death of tens of thousands of trees; and great forests such as the Black Forest in Germany are dying before our very eyes because of acid rain.

## Tree of Life or Death

There is within the Western tradition a deep-seated respect for trees. The tree has a central position. Trees are part of the drama of our redemption in Christianity.

The first tree is that of the knowledge of good and evil in the Garden of Eden. The violation of God's command to leave the tree alone is seen as the first action of disobedience by humanity which broke the harmonious relationship between us and God and us and the rest of nature.

The second tree is that which was cut down, cut apart and shaped to become the tree of death—the cross of the crucifixion. On this tree—shaped to an evil end by humanity—the Lord of Life was killed by us, a part of his creation. But through the resurrection, death was transformed into life and the possibility of our salvation arose.

Finally, in the vision of the Eternal City of God, in the book of Revelation, there is the tree of life, planted at the heart of the new city and under whose branches all shall live in harmony.

It is as though, through the model of our use of and relationship with trees, Christianity can highlight what has gone wrong and what can be redeemed, with regard to ourselves and God and ourselves and the rest of nature.

In Islam there is an ancient saying which captures our need for trees, namely, that wood cares for you from the cradle to the coffin! In Judaism the *Torah* forbids the destruction of fruit trees during a war;

> *When you besiege a city . . . you shall not destroy its trees . . . for you may eat of them but not cut them down. Are the trees in the fields men, that they should be besieged by you?*
>
> (Deuteronomy, 20:19)

Yet these attitudes, interesting as they are, do not really take us deep enough into the basic fact that, without trees, the planet will die, to all intents and purposes. The approaches above are all very well and, indeed, there is much within the Christian symbolism which could be and occasionally is creatively explored—the charred-wood cross of Coventry Cathedral, with its setting of the quote "Father forgive", is one example. Judaism also has developed a New Year festival for trees, when tree-planting takes place. But we need to have a wider approach. Hints of this appear in literature of our own century. A sense that the very life of the planet lies within the gift of the trees is captured powerfully in the final pages of C. S. Lewis's *Prince Caspian*, the fourth book in his *Narnia Chronicles*:

> *But almost before the Old Narnians were really warmed to their work they found the enemy giving way. Tough-looking warriors turned white, gazed in terror not on the Old Narnians but on something behind them, and then flung down their weapons, shrieking, 'The Wood! The Wood! The end of the world!'*
>
> *But soon neither their cries nor the sound of weapons could be heard any more, for both were drowned in the ocean-like roar of the Awakened Trees as they plunged through the ranks of Peter's army, and then on, in pursuit of the Telmarines. Have you ever stood at the edge of a great wood on a high ridge when a wild south-wester broke over it in full fury on an autumn evening? Imagine that sound. And then imagine that the wood,*

*instead of being fixed to one place, was rushing at you; and was no longer trees but huge people; yet still like trees because their long arms waved like branches and their heads tossed and leaves fell around them in showers. It was like that for the Telmarines. . . .*

(C. S. Lewis, *Prince Caspian*, Bodley Head, 1956, Penguin, 1962)

Perhaps we need to feel that the trees are our allies in the struggle to make life possible and worthwhile on earth—not just because they keep our atmosphere alive with oxygen, and provide the setting for much of the flora and fauna of the world, but because without them, we and all creation could barely survive.

When all is said and done, our approach to trees is probably still fundamentally utilitarian, even if we know that this is not sufficient. So let us look to other traditions where a different witness to trees has been a part and parcel of life.

## Dying for the trees

In the now quite desertified region of Rajasthan, in India, there is one area where the forest stands as tall and as strong as it always has done, thanks to the remarkable witness and lifestyle of a particular Hindu group.

Over five hundred years ago a guru known as Jambhaji Maharaj founded a sect of Hinduism called the Bishnoi. The word "Bishnoi" means "followers of the 29 Rules", and this explains the source of their strength. Jambhaji Maharaj gave his followers a set of rules, based upon the fundamentals of Hindu religion with its belief in the *atman*—the soul—which is reborn through countless births. For Maharaj, the key to escape from rebirth was non-violence—*ahimsha*, which was later to be made so famous by Mahatma Gandhi.

Basic to Jambhaji's teachings was respect for the natural environment, and especially for trees. As a young man, he lived through a terrible drought and famine. He saw the link between deforestation, which was going on even then, and the loss of fertility in the land. Therefore he forbade the taking of life—any

life at all, including tree life. Indeed, he made it a tenet of Bishnoi faith that the people should be willing to lay down their own lives to prevent the breaking of this rule. The Bishnoi settled in part of Rajasthan in the sixteenth century and, because of their adherence to *ahimsha*, the area was soon renowned for its forests and for the wildlife which ran, and indeed still runs, to the villages there whenever danger threatens.

In the mid-eighteenth century, the Bishnoi witness to their forests was tested to the full. A local Muslim ruler wanted trees to fuel his lime kilns. Having already wasted the areas nearest to the provincial capital of Rajasthan, he sent his men to chop down the trees of the Bishnoi. Forbidden by their rules to fight, the people literally clung to their trees, embracing the trunks in order to place themselves between the trees and the axes of the woodcutters and soldiers. Three hundred and sixty-three men, women and children were massacred, dying for their trees, before the ruler, realising that he was up against a group who actually meant what they preached, called off his men and left the woods and forests of the Bishnoi to these gentle yet determined people. Today a small temple marks the site of the massacre. More importantly, the rich forests of the area still stand, a living witness to the wisdom of the Bishnoi as, all around them, desertification gathers speed because of the twin demands of industry and population. In these woods live species such as the blackbuck, which once roamed all over the Indian sub-continent, but which now is only to be found in the Bishnoi forests.

The Bishnoi faith teaches a profound respect and veneration for the trees and other vegetation, as well as for the wildlife of the area. Linked by the *atman*, the divine spark within all life, the Bishnoi see trees as being of equal importance with human beings—hence their willingness to die for the trees, much as others might die defending the poor, children or the weak. They use the trees for fuel, of course, but only dead wood. And before any wood is burnt, it is checked to make sure that no insects which would die in the flames are still inside. Because the Bishnoi allow the forest to continue and to regenerate naturally, they have plenty of fuel, while outside, others hack down the very plants which will be needed to supply fuel.

The Bishnoi are not alone in their attitude to trees as being the equals of human life. Other Hindu- and Buddhist-inspired groups bear witness to the truth that there is a common thread of life linking all creation on the earth. Equally important is the fact which the Bishnoi bring to everyone's attention that, without the most profound respect for trees, we are in danger of destroying the very fabric of our world. That the massive rate of destruction of the forests is for very short-term financial goals only adds to the necessity of developing much more profound relationships with the trees. Nowhere is this to be seen more tragically than in the rain forests of the Amazon and in the story of the Yanomamo Indians.

## The Amazonian Indians

How long the Yanomamo have lived in the Amazon river basin and dwelt amongst its vast rain forests is unknown: certainly for hundreds of years, quite probably for thousands. Over this time they have evolved a lifestyle and beliefs which have made it possible for them to survive in the conditions of the forest. One of their creation myths captures their integral understanding of their relationship with both the trees and the wild creatures of the forest:

Once there lived Curare-woman and Original Jaguar. Now Jaguar was very fond of the taste of meat and one day he caught Waipili the frog. Original Jaguar made Curare-woman cut up Waipili and Jaguar devoured the frog. But Curare-woman saved two tadpoles called Omao and Soawe. She hid them away in a pot.

Curare-woman kept Omao and Soawe safe from Original Jaguar. The two grew stronger day by day, but Jaguar was still a threat to them. So they decided to get rid of Jaguar. One day, Omao fooled Jaguar into climbing a tree. The tree was cunningly held down by a strong vine. When Omao cut the vine, the tree was released and flung Jaguar into the air, killing him.

Now Omao was hungry because he did not know how to grow yucca. Only Lalagi-gi, the cosmic anaconda, knew how to grow plants. Although Omao was very frightened of Lalagi-gi,

he wanted to learn how to grow yucca. So he presented some meat to Lalagi-gi. In return, Lalagi-gi brought yucca cuttings, yams, maize and other things and showed Omao how to plant. Without Lalagi-gi, people would not know how to grow crops.

It was long, long ago that Omao created the Yanomamo ancestors. He decided to make them out of hardwood trees. But hardwood trees are difficult to find so he asked his brother Soawe to help him. However Soawe was very lazy, and finding it was difficult to find hardwoods, he cut down softwood trees instead.

When Omao returned he was very angry to find so few hardwood and so many softwood trees. "I was going to make humans from the hardwood trees," he said. "Then they could live forever, just casting off their old skins. I was going to make the anacondas from the softwood trees, so that they would be weak and die young." Omao was so angry that he made the people from the softwood trees, which is why people are weak and do not live forever. Then he made the anacondas from the tough bark of the hardwood trees, which is why anacondas shed their skins and live for such a long time. Omao was still angry, so he left the world. Way, way down the river he went to the bottom of the sky.

The sense of being kin to and yet lesser than the trees has meant that the Yanomamo have always lived within the boundaries of a world in which the trees are assumed to have the greater power and meaning. This is reflected in the lifestyle of the Yanomamo. Their spectacular communal ring huts (over a hundred feet wide and open to the sky in the middle) are built from branches of the trees. They dwell in them for a number of years, clearing the area around the village for small gardens. Then, when they have drawn enough on the land and vegetation in that area, they depart and start again. Within a few years there is little left to show that there was a village there. The dwelling place decays back into the jungle and the trees soon grow up again.

And this cycle has been going on for untold generations. It would have continued for further untold generations were it not for outsiders' greed and ignorance of the ways of the rain forest.

The rain forest is a very fragile eco-system. Its size and its apparent lushness give a false impression of tenacity and strength. But, in fact, the soil in rain forests is very thin, and it is only through the sheer denseness of the undergrowth that nutrients are fed back into the soil, thus enabling plants to grow and trees to arise. Destroy the tree cover, and with it the undergrowth, and the soil is soon washed away or, if farmed, exhausted. Then the desertification begins. The Yanomamo, relating to the trees as younger brother to older brother, understood this and adapted their lifestyle accordingly. The outsiders did not, and it never occurred to them to ask the Yanomamo!

In 1973 the Brazilian government promised land to millions of impoverished peasants. The land it gave them was forest bordering on the new roads driven through the Amazon. Thousands of the very poorest of the poor flocked to the Amazon area where they fell foul of the conmen, extortioners and the climate. Small strips of forest land were cleared and the first crop looked good. But within a few years the crops failed as the soil gave out. The peasants were again penniless and were then evicted. The land was now only fit for grazing, and even that could only be supported for a few years. However, the grazers moved in with vast herds of cattle raised primarily to supply the hamburger industry of North America. Soon they had turned the former forest area into a dust bowl. Meanwhile, loggers had also travelled up the new roads. Within less than a decade, they have smashed their way through vast areas of forest, reducing the total coverage by a half at least. In their wake came the cattle destined for the US hamburger market, who finished off the job of destruction.

At first the Yanomamo tried to resist this invasion of their land by legal means, but to no avail. Then there were skirmishes and then systematic attempts to destroy the Yanomamo by outsiders who left poisoned food, or clothes impregnated with disease which the Yanomamo had never encountered. There were—and still are—hunters who hunt and kill the Yanomamo. In the last decade the ages-old lifestyle and beliefs of the Yanomamo have been virtually destroyed. With them have gone the fertility and life-giving powers of the great trees and their eco-system. What has been lost CULTURALLY and therefore ENVIRONMENTALLY is of enormous significance for humanity and for all the species of the rain forest. The epitaph to the Yanomamo has been given in the words of one of their leaders, speaking in the early 1980s. What he said shows the fragility of our eco-system and of those belief systems which live in close harmony with nature, and sounds a warning which we ignore literally at our peril:

> *Everyone likes to give as well as to receive. No-one wishes only to receive all the time. We have taken much from your culture . . . I wish you had taken something from our culture . . . for there were some good and beautiful things in it.*

## The Festival of Trees

Finally, in this consideration of trees, let us return to a faith which I touched upon briefly earlier: Judaism. For here is an interesting example of a tradition rediscovered and adapted for present-day needs.

The core teachings of Judaism are found within the *Torah*—the first five books of the Bible, commonly ascribed to Moses—and the *Talmud*—the collection of rabbinical commentaries on the *Torah*. Within the *Talmud* there are countless stories which bear witness to the centrality of trees in Jewish life. One of the earliest of these, relating to the *Torah* account in Genesis of the creation of man and the Garden of Eden, conveys a fundamental message about co-existence:

> *Adam walked in the Garden on the first day. He smelled wonderful scents and enjoyed the beautiful sight. The aroma of the ripening fruit drew him to the trees. He reached for an apricot that hung from a branch. The fruit lifted itself so that he could not touch it. He reached for a pomegranate. The fruit evaded his hand. Then a voice spoke. 'Till the soil and care for the trees and then you may eat.'*

This is the fundamental wisdom about trees which has lain within the Jewish faith: that humanity and trees should co-exist under God, to the benefit of both, the trees providing food, shelter and materials and humanity caring for and nurturing the trees. A further insight into the traditional teachings of Judaism with regard to trees is afforded by this story, also from the *Talmud*:

> *A wise rabbi was walking down a road when he saw a man planting a tree. The rabbi asked him, 'How many years will it take for this tree to bear fruit?' The man answered that it would take seventy years. The rabbi asked 'Are you so fit and strong that you expect to live that long and eat of its fruit?' The man answered, 'I found a fruitful world because my forefathers planted for me. So I will do the same for my children.'*

The planting of and caring for trees illustrate the Jewish belief that whilst the fruits of this earth are here for us to enjoy, we have to look not just to our own needs but to the needs of those who will come after us. In following this belief, of course, Judaism teaches the basic principles of good tree husbandry and points to the inter-relationship between ourselves and the trees and forests which can so easily be taken for granted. As we saw in Chapter 1, Judaism views time and history (on the whole) as linear. There is also the hope of the Messiah, who will come to end all suffering and institute the reign of the Lord. Yet one of the Talmudic texts says, "If a man comes to you while you are planting a tree and says, 'Come quickly for the Messiah has arrived', first finish planting the tree and then go and see the Messiah." In other words, the Messianic age may be about to happen, but you still have a duty to your children's children and to nature to ensure that, if the Messiah has not yet come, the created world will continue to flourish and feed your descendants.

But how has this wisdom of the *Torah* and the *Talmud* expressed itself in Jewish life? For many centuries—indeed, even millenia—the Jews have not been in a position to own or control land. They have thus had little opportunity to put into practice what their teachings tell them. Nevertheless, throughout the centuries, there has been a minor festival known as Tu B'Shevat, which means the New Year for Trees. When Judaism was effectively landless, the opportunities for planting trees were very limited, but early in this century, as the hope of returning to the Holy Land grew, with the rise of Zionism and the development of kibbutzim, Tu B'Shevat came to be of considerably greater importance. It has now become a time when families and congregations world-wide pay for trees to be planted. Usually this means that the trees are planted in Israel, especially since the formation of the State of Israel, but it is also the case that trees are planted in the neighbourhoods where the families and congregations live. The restoration of practical action to the festival of the New Year for Trees has given impetus to the afforestation programme of Israel and this has been part of the reason for the programme's success. Whilst, for instance, Saudi Arabia has also made extraordinary advances in afforesting its desert areas, there has not been the same sense there of participation and involvement as Tu B'Shevat has afforded to the Jewish world. The festival has brought the profound insights of the *Torah* and *Talmud* to a practical enactment and denouement.

Yet here is an interesting example of interaction between cultures. For the rise of Zionism was only one reason behind the growth of interest in the ancient but formerly little observed festival of Tu B'Shevat. Another reason was the rise of environmental awareness, not least with regard to trees. It was, in fact, the development of the tree-planting movement, founded in the mid-1920s, which fused with the ancient tradition and with the emerging new reality of Zionism to form a response to the environment which is now seen as an automatic and natural reflection of Judaism's deepest teachings with regard to nature. This is an important point to note. Within all the faiths there are immensely powerful symbols, festivals and teachings. That they may have lain dormant for centuries is no reason to go on ignoring them or for considering them incapable of development, as we shall see later in this book.

But let us turn to yet another set of perceptions: what is the diversity of response which cultures have made to the existence of animals?

## The animals

When people wish to dismiss the intellectual world of the Middle

Ages, and in particular when they wish to ridicule the efforts of the theologians and scholars of the ecclesiastical world of mediaeval Christendom, they usually cite two cases which they believe highlight the aridity of debate and thinking of that period: "How many angels can dance on the point of a needle?" and "Do animals have souls?". The fact that so many of our contemporaries in the world of philosophy, as well as in the wider intellectual community, can still find the latter laughable shows how culturally conditioned we are. For, in many cultures, that debate is not seen as being at all meaningless, whilst, in others, animals are believed without doubt to have souls—hence there *is* no debate. Meanwhile, here in the UK, it is still possible for respected philosophers to exclaim that, whereas human beings have rights (the modern equivalent of souls in much thought!), which are ironically called at times "natural rights" or, more honestly, "human rights", animals have no rights. Says who? Given that the very concept of rights did not exist until recently, why have we in the West decided that they apply only to us and not to the rest of creation? This is an issue which will be examined later. I mention it here to show how very deeply ingrained within Western culture is the assumption that animals have no rights, or souls. This, I would argue, has actually led us to commit more acts of violence against the rest of the animal world than any other factor. So let us look at how other cultures view the animal world.

## Sacred cows

Gandhi said that the greatest gift which Hinduism could give to the world was the example of the sacred cow. "Cow protection," he said, "to me is one of the most wonderful phenomena in all human evolution, for it takes the human being beyond his species. The cow to me means the entire sub-human world. Man through the cow is enjoined to realise his identity with all that lives. . . . The cow is a poem of pity. . . . Protection of the cow means protection of the whole dumb creation of God."

Gandhi was talking here to a non-Hindu audience; the language he uses reflects his attempt to span two cultures. To discover the heart of what he meant we need to look at the core belief of Hinduism. Hindus believe that all life is linked through the existence in all life-forms of a soul, or the *atman*, as it is properly known. While the outward form, the physical appearance, changes—from tree or animal, bird or reptile or human—the *atman* remains the same, as it seeks to rejoin the Divine. This belief means that human beings, far from seeing themselves as set apart from the rest of creation, should, if endowed with true understanding, see themselves on a par with all other forms of life, higher or lower as they may appear. This is well expressed in the *Bhagavad Gita*, the main scripture of Hinduism. In Chapter 5, Lord Krishna teaches Arjuna that "The wise look upon a Brahman full of learning and humility, a cow, an elephant, a dog and a low caste dog-eater as alike." Because of the spark of the Divine within all life, all life is essentially and ultimately of the same true nature. The outward manifestations—the physical clothing of the *atman*—are, in the end, irrelevant.

In Hindu thought, there are thousands of rebirths to be experienced as the *atman* seeks to progress to the point of release and return to the Divine. That progress depends primarily on the development of the *atman*'s *karma*—that is to say, the cumulative effects of actions of either good or bad behaviour. The *atman* has to be reborn while there are still "left-over" effects from the actions of previous lives. *Karma* is these effects. Until it has ceased, until there is no longer any retribution or result of previous actions, the *atman* cannot achieve release. The different levels of life—vegetable, simple animal life, complex animal life, human beings, demi-gods—reflect the progressive stages of spiritual growth. It is possible to regress in the chain and to revert from being a human being to being a dog, for instance. Today, this is often explained in semi-psychological terms. If someone behaves like a pig or is aggressive like a tiger or destructive like a rat, then he or she will be reborn in that condition.

The idea of *karma* has many important ecological and moral lessons. In Hindu thought, what fuels the constant rebirth of souls is the continuing, post-death effects of actions committed during a given life-time or life-times. All actions have consequences. If I harm a person, he or she will harbour a grudge against me and seek some opportunity of revenge. This, in turn, will affect that person's relationships with others, and so on and so on. Each action leads to a chain of consequences which do not cease at death but have to be resolved or worked through in the next rebirth. The aim of Hindu meditation and study is to reduce the *karma* which one carries from one life to another. This can be done through good actions or, more importantly, through right mind and behaviour. Let us hear from the *Vedas* to recall the strength of belief in the *atman*—the Divine within all—as the basis of understanding the role of *karma*:

*The loving sage beholds that Being, hidden in mystery,*
*wherein the universe comes to have one home:*
*Therein unites and therefrom emanates the whole:*
*The Omnipresent One is warp and woof in created beings.*

(Yajurveda 32.8)

If the Omnipresent One is in all created beings, then to kill another being is to attack the Divine. The karmic consequences of this are enormous and this is why so many Hindus are vegetarian. This is the basis of *ahimsha*—non-harming, to put it at its most precise.

The concept of the unity of all life finds symbolic and visual expression in the gods and goddesses of Hinduism and their animal companions. Hinduism is rich in symbols and imagery depicting some of the aspects of the Divine. For instance, the three main attributes of the Divine are captured in the three Lords: Lord Brahma who creates each universe and world—he faces in all four directions, Lord of all aspects of his creation; Lord Vishnu who sustains them—for instance, his neck is always coloured blue because he swallowed a terrible poison which threatened to destroy the universe; and Lord Shiva who both destroys and restores and is often depicted as Lord of the Dance in the famous circle statue. Each of the gods and goddesses has an animal or creature which is pictured as being the deity's constant companion. Thus Brahma has a wildgoose, Vishnu an eagle, Shiva a serpent and a bull, Durga a lion, and so on. Hinduism also has its animal deities. The two most famous and enormously popular ones are Ganesha, the elephant-headed god of good fortune, and Hanuman, the warrior monkey who was instrumental in helping Rama find his wife Sita and in defeating the ten-headed demon, Ravana, who had abducted her. Hindu mythology also abounds with tales of animal heroes.

Many Hindus today feel that, despite all this, the Hindu treatment of nature, and especially of animals, leaves much to be desired. Drs Dwivedi and Tiwari put it very bluntly. Writing as Hindu believers and, in Dr Dwivedi's case, as a social scientist deeply concerned with the environment, they ask:

> *Why has Hindu religion been unable to protect and preserve the ancient value which encouraged respect and due regard to God's creation? Was it not possible for Hindu culture to fight against the obsession of growth, consumption and consumerism? Could not the religion prepare man to control his aggressive, competitive and possessive individualism which gave rise to exploitative tendencies? Why was the concept of divinity in nature, emphasized through various incarnations of God and described by the Hindu patron saint Dattatreya, not maintained over the centuries?*
>
> (*Environmental Crisis and Hindu Religion*, Gitanjali Publishing House, New Delhi, 1987)

The challenge laid before Hinduism by writers such as these is just beginning to be answered. As the writers go on to show in their book, there are many resources within Hinduism which, if developed, could begin to answer those questions.

Yet despite the loss for many of an overall sense of responsibility towards all other *atmans*, as is seen in the growth of hunting; and despite the encroachment of other world views which have undercut the foundations of Hindu beliefs, it is still the case that within the continuing traditions of the faith there are practices which illustrate the *ahimsha* values of non-violence towards all life which also form the basis of the Bishnoi belief. For instance, in many villages the practice is still followed of putting out grain for the rats in the grain store. Studies by Western ecologists seem to support the villagers' claim that in this way the rats are prevented from eating the stored grain and the population of rats is self-controlling and never grows beyond a certain level. They point to places where this centuries-old, *ahimsha* way of dealing with rats has been dropped, in favour of trapping them or poisoning them. There the rat population regenerates itself much faster, to keep up with the additional deaths caused by trapping or poisoning, and therefore the level of damage remains constant. The side-effects of laying poison and the damage which is now done to the stored grain (thus increasing instances of illness amongst those who later consume contaminated grain) are seen as karmic retribution arising from the killing of other sentient beings. The *ahimsha* principle, as a part of *karma*, is the basis for Hindu attitudes to animals, which are so clearly illustrated by the practical treatment of and respect for the cow.

There are very pragmatic grounds for not killing cows. Alive, they provide much more than dead! Hindus put it much more pleasantly. They see the cow as Mother, for she provides milk, fuel (dung), fertiliser, medicine (urine) and, when she dies, leather for various purposes. If you imagine this practical attitude fused with the ideas of the Divine in all life, the *atman* and *karma*, you will begin to understand why cows wander the main roads of India—rural and urban—completely safe from harm or molestation. You can also begin to glimpse what Gandhi was saying when he saw within the fundamental respect afforded to cows a hint of the depth of Hindu attitudes towards other life-forms which could be such an important pointer for other cultures.

## The harmlessness of the Jains

Over two thousand five hundred years ago Hinduism spawned a new faith. Drawing upon many of the core beliefs of Hinduism, it developed its own distinct teachings, lifestyle and authorities. The faith is known as Jainism, from the word "*jinas*" meaning "those who have overcome", and its teachings are based upon belief in the 24 *Tithankaras*—those who had overcome the world of the physical and attained true spiritual status. The Jains are particularly well-known for their quite extraordinary reverence for all forms of life. They are total vegetarians and it is from them that the concept of *ahimsha* first arose.

In Jain cosmology all life has feeling. All existence is classified into five categories, known as the One to Five Sense Categories. The one-sensed, so called because, according to Jain thought, they experience only feeling, are the smallest animate particles of earth, water, fire, wind and plants. Even at this most basic level, each particle has a soul dwelling within it and is therefore to be respected. The other four levels rise up through the various forms of life, from the simplest to the most complex. Unlike Hinduism, but like Buddhism, which arose from the same area at the same time, Jainism has a corpus of central teachings which are passed on by a community of monks and nuns. Such are the reverence for all feeling life, and the authority of the command not to violate any feeling being, that monks and nuns carry with them two instruments to ensure that they do the least harm to sentient beings. The first is a *rayaharar* or *paya-pumchana*, a hand brush formed of twigs or soft wool, which is used to clear the ground before a monk or nun steps on, or rests anything upon, it. The brush removes all creatures which might otherwise be harmed or killed by the action of the monk or nun. The second artefect the monk or nun must carry is the *muha-pottiya*, a napkin or handkerchief. It has two functions. When a monk or nun is travelling, it is worn over the mouth, to prevent the breathing in of insects or dust, which are classified as alive under the One to Five Senses classification. Its second use is to gently clear the area where a book or alms bowl or any other object is to be laid and which again might harm a living being.

For laypeople in Jainism, the teachings about the value of all life have been specifically set forth in the vows which are binding upon them. These fall into three categories, namely, the small vows, the additional vows and the strengthening vows. The first of the small vows is to abstain from gross offences, which might lead to death, against living matter. In the additional vows, the layperson is forbidden to engage in trades which endanger living matter. Amongst these trades—which give us a clear idea of the extent of the Jain concept of living matter—are charcoal burning, ivory and lacquer trading, the pressing of fruit kernels, the draining of swamps, and so on. To this day, Jains are to be found in only a very small number of trades which do not involve harming living creatures.

The monastic writings and codes are full of regulations designed to ensure that no harm is done to any living creature. For instance, it is recommended that people do not move about after dark because it will be more difficult for them to avoid stepping on a living creature. The whole lifestyle and teaching of the Jains are pervaded by a sense of respect for the right to exist of other souls, other beings with feelings (including dust). This is not just a nice idea. It is actually practised.

The realities of Jain life under these rules make it very circumscribed and slow, and so it does not appeal to many in the West. However, it does show how respect for living beings, if translated into practice, will mean a profound change in behaviour, outlook and values.

## Of concepts and conceits

In this chapter I have tried to show that there are other ways of viewing life than the ways with which we are most familiar. As I have said earlier, we seem to lack the conceptual capacity to rethink our fundamental relationships with the natural world. We seem to feel that all we can do is tinker with the edges, whilst leaving unchallenged what we often acknowledge to be essentially self-defeating concepts. But this need not be so. There are other models of reality, other visions of what life is really about, and other lifestyles arising from these, which can offer us, regardless of our belief system, a chance to rethink various dimensions of our relationship with nature.

As stated at the beginning of this chapter, I am not trying to turn everyone into an Australian aboriginal or a Jain monk! What I am saying is that most of our major conceptual systems have become distorted and incapable on their own of delivering us from our own destruction or gross abuse of the very planet upon which we seek to live. Some of the factors in this crisis of the mind have been explored at the end of Chapter 1 and in Chapter 2. I now want to look at what the major faiths have to say in general to us about how we understand the world and how we should respond to it. For within the great traditions there are many vital and profound insights which, together with some of the beliefs which we have looked at in this chapter, may be able to help us fashion for ourselves a workable perceptual model of the natural world and our role within it. It is to this role that I now wish to turn, using it as the key for unlocking what each faith has to say about how we should perceive and relate to nature.

# 4

# Returning to Roots

In the previous chapter we looked at a wide range of belief systems. Many of them are what might be called "indigenous" belief systems: that is to say, they are systems which have never seen themselves, nor sought to be seen, as universal, or as having universal significance. They have developed in certain localities and that is where they function. In some cases, remove them from the particular geographical location where they were formed, and they die. Yet contained within them, precisely because they are rooted in certain eco-systems, are insights of tremendous importance for any other people who wish to share the environment they inhabit. I would also argue that there are certain insights which, whilst not immediately applicable to other contexts, raise major questions or alternative ways of thinking to help clear the intellectual and perceptual constipation from which so many of us suffer.

A recent project report by the WWF, National Geographic Society and National Science Foundation, about the Kayapo Indians in the Brazilian Amazon, highlights this idea. A team of scientists has been working with the Kayapo Indians over the last five years. Their report describes how, following traditional methods codified by myths, legends and rituals, the Kayapo Indians plant certain species together, calling them "friends that grow together". The scientists found that, in fact, the plants do grow better together and that the Indians had discovered for themselves the fact of synergistic plants—plants that respond better when planted with certain other species.

To protect their crops, the Indians have developed a most effective and ecologically harmless system. The greatest threat to crops in the forest is from leaf-cutter ants. The main foes of leaf-cutter ants are predatory insects, the foremost of which are parasitic wasps. Parasitic wasps like to nest in certain types of banana tree. So the Kayapo Indians, following an old legend, plant these types of banana tree around the edges of their fields as well as amongst the crops, thus ensuring a domestic force of wasps to deal with the ants.

The Kayapo Indians revere a particular kind of electric eel which lives in deep ponds. The eel is believed to live off minnows, and so the Indians' culture teaches them not to fish where they see spawning fish or minnows. This has ensured that the fish are able to mature, and has kept the aquatic food chain of the river from unnecessary disruption.

All these examples reinforce what we saw in different ways in Chapter 3: that rooted in different beliefs there are insights of both a conceptual and a pragmatic nature, which have a great deal to offer to us. However, Dr Posey, leader of the project team, says that "the most formidable barrier" to improving ecological and development methods by learning from the Kayapo is "the scientist's lack of credence in folk specialists. This manifests itself in a reluctance to allow the informant to lead the researcher into areas of research that the native chooses."

## Science and religion

The problem of environmentalists not taking seriously other world views is not confined to their response to indigenous traditions. The same attitude has bedevilled conservation's relationship with the major universal faiths. (By this I mean the faiths which see themselves as having a message for humanity at large, even if they do not always see that this necessitates the conversion of all people to their faith.) When it arose in the 1950s, conservation, needing like all new movements a sense of authority and a series of beliefs upon which to be based, turned to the scientific, secular model. It has therefore seen itself as heir to science in the presumed old battle between science and religion. Dr Posey's remark quoted earlier reflects what damage this has done. At the level of the interaction between conservation and the major faiths the conflict has created a mighty abyss, across which it was deemed not wise to step. Conservationists with religious faith kept the two worlds—professional and personal—apart.

The questions of what actually really divides religion and science and whether the battles fought were ones of language rather than of substantive content, are not within the scope of this book. Excellent studies have been written on this area, such as Arthur Peacocke's *Creation and the World of Science* (Oxford University Press, 1979) or David Lindberg and Ronald Number's *God and Nature* (University of California Press, 1986) and such works warrant close attention. What is important for our subject is that the old battle lines have begun to crumble and there is a great deal of fruitful interchange between science and religion. But science still has a lot of chips on its shoulder which it needs to be rid of with regard to religion.

An interesting point is made about the relationship between conservation and religion in the preface to the new edition of Jim Lovelock's book, *Gaia—a new look at life on earth.* In this important book, Lovelock argues that the earth itself should be seen and related to as a living being, a single organism, which is capable of growth and development and which defines and maintains the conditions necessary for its own survival. Again we run up against humanity as the (if you'll pardon the phrase) "fly in the ointment", and the book argues powerfully for rethinking our relationship with earth. More of this later. In his new preface Lovelock remarks:

> *Things have taken a strange turn in recent years; almost the full circle from Galileo's famous struggle with the theological establishment. It is the scientific establishment that now forbids heresy. I had a faint hope that 'Gaia' might be denounced from the pulpit; instead I was asked to deliver a sermon on 'Gaia' at the Cathedral of St John the Divine in New York. By contrast 'Gaia' was condemned as teleological by my peers and the journals 'Nature' and 'Science' would not publish papers on the subject.*
>
> (Lovelock, *Gaia—a new look at life on earth*, Oxford University Press, 1979, reprinted 1987)

It is perhaps time to bury the hatchet; for both religion and science to admit their need of each other and for there to be a greater openness to new ideas in both camps.

## Conversion for conservation

By dwelling in the outdated concepts of late nineteenth-century scientific world views conservationists cut themselves off from some of the most powerful potential allies in the struggle to change the hearts, minds and behaviour of people. The major religions are enormously influential. They are also in certain cases the original sources of some of the best as well as the worst concepts which are currently to be found in secular thought as expressed in various forms. The conservation movement is the poorer for not involving the religious groups; the religious groups are the poorer for not having been prodded into putting into action their teachings on conservation.

Then, in 1986, a strange thing happened which has radically changed the scene. Early that year, HRH Prince Philip, as President of WWF International, invited representatives of the five major faiths (Buddhism, Christianity, Hinduism, Islam and Judaism) to come on pilgrimage to Assisi with representatives of the major conservation bodies, to celebrate the twenty-fifth anniversary of WWF. The invitation was made in order that each group could present its understanding and vision of our relationship with nature, and learn from the other groups. The response from the five world faiths was extraordinary and all sent leading figures, representing structures within each faith which are capable of reaching millions upon millions of the faithful. Furthermore, other faiths also came, from the Baha'i faith with its four and a half million members, through the Jains with their three and a half million members, to representatives of major cultures such as the Maoris and native North American Indians.

At the end of the historic meeting in the town of St Francis there was an unprecedented interfaith ceremony, at the culmination of which a new alliance between religions and conservation was announced. Prince Philip summed up what it meant:

> *We came to Assisi to find vision and hope. Vision to discover a new and caring relationship with the rest of our living world, and hope that the destruction of nature can be stopped before all is wasted and lost.*
>
> *I believe that today, in this famous shrine of the saint of ecology, a new and powerful alliance has been forged between the*

*forces of religion and the forces of conservation. I am convinced that secular conservation has learnt to see the problems of the natural world from a different perspective and, I hope and believe, that the spiritual leaders have learnt that the natural world of Creation cannot be saved without their active involvement. Neither can ever be quite the same again.*

(*Religion and Nature Interfaith Ceremony*, published by WWF International, Gland, 1986)

This new alliance was followed by the Declarations of Assisi. For the first time in history, five of the world's major faiths publicly and in print stated where they stood on the issue of care for or in nature. Each faith's Declaration bore witness to the specific insights and visions held true by that particular faith. Thus there are Buddhist, Christian, Hindu, Jewish and Muslim Declarations of Assisi. In 1987 a sixth Declaration was made by the Baha'i faith. In certain cases, the call to prepare a Declaration which would be announced at Assisi required the particular faith, for the first time ever, to sit down and try to put into words exactly what it had to say about ecology and nature and conservation. (Each faith was limited to using no more than six sides of A4 paper, to ensure that the documents would be brief and to the point!) The results were mixed, but the significance considerable. Since then each of the faiths has returned to its own faithful and has sought in different ways to explore in greater detail what it has to offer in the quest for a better understanding of, attitude towards and treatment of the rest of nature. It is as though the challenge thrown down, ironically, by a secular body has struck a chord within each of the major faiths.

Vice versa, the dramatic movement of the religions on to the scene of conservation has led to considerable rethinking by the secular conservationists. They have had to come to terms with the fact that the way they see the world, and thus conservation, is conditioned by the culture and belief system in which they live. This means that, quite often, the way secular conservationists have tackled problems has led to failure because they were too blinkered to see alternative approaches. There has also been a challenge by the faiths—the majority of whose members are neither white nor Western—to the implicit and at times explicit racism which has marred and obstructed the work of international conservation bodies. Finally, the ideological links between Western conservation and Western capitalism and neocolonialism have been sharply criticised by religion—which, by its very nature, transcends such groupings—and this has led some conservationists to wonder if they have not, by default, supped too much with the Devil. The religious involvement in conservation, raising, as it does, issues of justice and peace, of cultural imperialism and consumption, of values and norms, is still far from popular in certain areas of the conservation world. But this is only to be expected. Traditional believers in any belief system which they hold to be really true are always loath to admit that anyone else might have an equally valid perspective on the world. The conservation movement is behaving like any other belief system which suddenly finds it lives in a multicultural world.

In earlier chapters we saw the good, the bad and, at times, the indifferent attitudes which certain faiths have engendered towards the natural world. We have seen how some groups within major faiths have fallen under the spell of false beliefs or of false teleologies. But, as argued at the beginning of Chapter 3, any concept of faiths which does not take into account interaction and development is dealing with only a husk of religion. The response of the major faiths to the WWF Assisi invitation and the consequent exploration of their own traditions have begun to show not just what might happen in each faith's relationship with nature, but what has in fact been going on amongst its more thoughtful members for years, without being recognised or understood until recently.

I now want to look at some of the ways in which the major faiths have found insights about nature in their own traditions and at how this is leading them to seek to develop new relationships with the natural world. As before, with the examples of diverse responses to specific natural phenomena, I am not seeking to argue that everyone should become a Buddhist or a Christian, although I can think of a few cases where this would be immensely helpful! Rather, I am wanting to see what variety of models of overall understanding there are within the major faiths. What understanding do these have for us to draw on—together with the indigenous, the ideological and the scientific systems—in the struggle for conservation? All these are essential to help us find the conceptual and symbolic resources which we need at times, quite literally, to "see" our way through the mess we have made and are making of this planet.

## Buddhism

In Chapter 2 we touched on the central Buddhist precept of non-violence, and on the model of compassion which is found in various forms of Buddhism. This model is beautifully captured in the Vow of the Bodhisattva, from the sixth to the seventh century CE. The Vow was taken for all life, not just the human one.

> *A Bodhisattva resolves: I take upon myself the burden of all sufferings, I am resolved to do so, I will endure it. I do not turn or run away, do not tremble, am not terrified, nor afraid, do not turn back or despair.*
>
> *And why? At all costs I must bear the burden of all beings, in that I do not follow my own inclinations. I have made the vow to save all beings. All beings I must set free. The whole world of living beings I must rescue, from the terrors of birth, of old age, of sickness, of death and rebirth, of all kinds of moral offence, of all states of woe, of the whole cycle of birth-and-death, of the jungle of false views, of the loss of wholesome dharmas [teachings], of the concomitants of ignorance—from all these terrors I must rescue all beings. . . . I walk so that the kingdom of unsurpassed cognition is built up for all beings. My endeavours do not merely aim at my own deliverance. For with the help of the boat of the thought of all-knowledge, I must rescue all these beings from the stream of Samsara [rebirth and suffering], which is so difficult to cross, I must pull them back from the great precipice, I must free them from all calamities, I must ferry them across the stream of Samsara. I myself must grapple with the whole mass of suffering of all beings. To the limit of endurance I will experience in all the states of woe, found in any world system, all the abodes of suffering. And I must not cheat all beings out of my store of merit. I am resolved to abide in each*

*single state of woe for numberless aeons; and so I will help all beings to freedom, in all states of woe that may be found in any world system whatsoever.*

(Shantideva's Sikshasamuccaya 280–81, Vajradhvaja Sutra)

This vision of compassionate care has been lived out in practice by the community of monks, the *Sangha*. Their compassion for all life has meant that temple grounds and temples have always been places where wildlife was safe from hunters. In many parts of Asia to this day it is within the environs of temples, monasteries and sacred mountains that endangered species still survive, protected by the compassion of the monks and the reverence of laypeople towards such holy sites. Indeed, conservationists have begun to appreciate the importance ecologically of Buddhist sites in places such as Thailand or Sri Lanka. The sacred nature of such sites has, by accident, permitted the survival of certain species, as well as providing examples of balanced human interaction with nature.

However, this sacred sanctity has been a passive concept, one which happened by chance to have beneficial ecological spin-offs. In recent years the *Sangha* has begun to examine its role in caring for the natural world, the world of sentient beings. Projects have been established, such as the joint Thai and Tibetan Buddhist "Perceptions of Nature" project which has brought together senior scholars to examine the Buddhist scriptures and to publish studies of the core teachings of Buddhism with regard to nature. Through such study, the monks have realised that they should turn their passive care of nature into an active, teaching, preaching and practical care. The academic studies are now being reworked to provide educational material for Buddhist schools in various parts of the East. For instance, how prophetic and wise is this extract from the stories of the Buddha's previous lives, the Jataka stories:

*Come back O Tigers! to the woods again,*
*And let it not be levelled with the plain;*
*For without you, the axe will lay it low;*
*You, without it, for ever homeless go.*

(*The Jataka* Vol. II, ed. Prof. E. B. Cowell, The Pali Text Society, London, 1957)

Certain monks have decided to turn the passive belief in the sacredness of life within the monastery grounds into an active one of taking the concept of compassion and care out to the villagers. For instance, in northern Thailand, the abbot of one of the major monasteries has led the local villagers in a scheme of re-afforestation which is slowly but surely bringing life back to the hills and woods and restoring the water-table levels. As a forest monk of the Thai tradition, the abbot, Acharn Pongsak, spends many weeks alone, meditating in the forest. Over the years he has watched as the forested areas of Thailand have diminished. He also watched as the streams and rivers flowing from the now denuded hills shrank and died. In his area, five of the eight streams had ceased to flow, as the rainwater, rather than being absorbed by the trees and forest and drawn into the water table, now ran off the barren hills and caused flash floods. He also noticed the demise of wildlife and saw that this related to the destruction of their habitat. Motivated initially by Buddhist teachings, such as compassion, the common link in all life, the Acharn began to organise the villagers into replanting trees and into opposing the loggers and forestry officials who, sadly, were more interested in making private profits than in caring for the forests. And over the years he has begun to see life returning to the hills, and waters to the streams. The villagers, whose crops were failing through lack of water, can see the positive benefits of planting trees and recreating the habitats of the wild creatures—of putting compassion into action, for, in true karmic fashion, they reap the benefits of such action. Acharn Pongsak puts well what he and the others have learnt, as Buddhists, from this venture:

> *Not all morality is covered by the five, eight, ten or 227 Buddhist precepts. There is morality also in recognising the benefits we owe to nature. This is a part of the true morality. If we could always keep an awareness in some part of our minds of a sense of gratitude to nature, then we could say we had gained an understanding of the essence of Buddhist morality.*

> (Quoted in *The New Road*, the bulletin of the WWF Network on Conservation and Religion, Issue 2, Spring 1987)

In other parts of the world, such as Sri Lanka and Japan, the

Buddhist witness is also being made active in a similar way. The process of reflection comes over in the opening of the Buddhist Declaration of Assisi:

> *In the words of the Buddha himself: 'Because the cause was there, the consequences followed; because the cause is there, the effects will follow.' These few words present the inter-relationship between cause (karma) and its effects. It goes a step further and shows that happiness and suffering do not simply come about by chance or irrelevant causes. There is a natural relationship between a cause and its resulting consequence in the physical world. In the life of sentient beings too, including animals, there is a similar relationship of positive causes bringing about happiness and negative actions causing negative consequences. Therefore a human undertaking motivated by a healthy and positive attitude constitutes one of the most important causes of happiness, while undertakings generated through ignorance and negative attitude bring about suffering and misery. And this positive human attitude is, in the final analysis, rooted in genuine and unselfish compassion and loving kindness that seeks to bring about light and happiness for all sentient beings. Hence Buddhism is a religion of love, understanding and compassion, and committed towards the ideal of non-violence. As such it also attaches great importance to wildlife and the protection of the environment on which every being in this world depends for survival.*
>
> (*The Assisi Declarations*, published by WWF International, Gland, 1986)

Compassion in Buddhism is a motive standing in its own right. It is not linked to any fear of the End or any judgment. Rather, it is linked to a belief, as is stated above, that your actions return to you and affect you as much as those whom you have affected. The belief in rebirths, through which you work off the effects of your *karma*, has led to a fascinating series of stories about the different rebirths of the historical Buddha, Gautama. Before he reached the state of being the Buddha, the Enlightened One, he passed through countless rebirths and through all the stages of existence. Therefore, the stories, known as the Jataka tales, tell of him as a bird, an elephant, a monkey, a tree, etc. In all these manifestations he shows compassion to all creatures and is often pictured laying down his own life for the others in his flock or herd. Through all these stories comes a very clear message that hunting and harming other sentient beings are evil.

Take, for instance, the story of the future Buddha's birth as a deer. He was incarnated as a most beautiful deer and, when he grew to maturity, he was made the leader of the herd of some five hundred. In the same forest there lived another magnificent stag, also leader of a large herd. Both of the leaders were wise and caring.

Unfortunately, the king of nearby Benaras loved venison. Every day he sent his people into the forest to hunt and take a deer. Soon the people began to grumble, for the effort of hunting was taking them away from their work on the fields. They came up, instead, with a clever idea. They built a huge corral and herded the two groups of deer into it. Now the king's butcher had only to go to the corral in order to take the meat for the king.

The king was delighted, but gave orders that the two magnificent stags were not to be harmed. These two leaders decided that one deer per day would be chosen from each herd alternately, to supply the king. The deer to die was chosen by lot. One day, the lot fell upon a young pregnant doe. In tears she went to Branch, the second stag, and begged that she be released and another take her place. Branch refused, saying that he could not ask another deer to take her place. So she turned to the future Buddha, leader of the other herd. He promised her that a substitute would be found.

When the butcher came the next day, the future Buddha came forward and laid his head upon the block. The butcher refused to kill him and the future Buddha refused to move. The king was called and asked the stag why he was volunteering to give up his own life. The stag explained that he could not ask another deer to give up his life for the pregnant doe, and so he had to take her place himself.

The king was deeply moved and said that, even amongst human beings, he had never seen such compassion. He spared the life of the stag and the doe. However, the future Buddha then asked the king to extend his compassion to all the deer.

The king agreed. The future Buddha pushed the king further and further until he extracted from him a promise never to hunt or harm any of the creatures of the forest, the birds of the air, or the fish of the waters.

The text of the story then continues:

*Having converted the king from the violent ways of a hunter to the way of compassion and non-injury to any form of life, which is the first of the five great rules of morality, the golden stag continued to preach to the king about the other virtues.*

For centuries much of Buddhism has quietly borne witness to this sense of compassion and interrelatedness. But, in recent years, the pace of change in Buddhist countries has been dramatically increased as a result of the exploitation of natural resources by multi-nationals and national governments. The older passive witness of Buddhism is now responding to this by taking the message out and by actively working to establish or re-establish a Buddhistic balance with nature.

## Christianity

In Christianity the debate about nature has been going on since Lynn White launched his attack (in an article published in *Science*, Vol. 155, 1967) on Christianity as the root cause of our current environmental crisis. This took place in the late 1960s and coincided with the tumultuous events of the student riots and activism of that period. Radical Christians were in the vanguard of much of this, and issues of the environment were high on the agenda. For instance, both the World Council of Churches and the World Student Christian Federation made it an area of study and debate within their own programmes.

In the more quiescent 1970s the debate died down at a public level, though at an academic and hierarchical level (i.e. at synods and Bishops' Councils, etc) it continued. This is very much the case today, except that a growing awareness has arisen that Christianity does need to put its own house in order, not least through being in contact with other belief systems.

The core of the dilemma is that, if one takes the traditional understanding of the Bible and of the Church Fathers, Christianity does have a very human-centred world view. The witness of many saints and ordinary people motivated by the Christian Gospel down the ages that all of life is important to God is still having to vie for attention with the more established view of Christianity and nature. That Christianity, in certain forms, has given rise to highly exploitative types of society or attitudes is beyond question; witness the attitudes of both the Catholic conquistadors and the Calvinist colonisers of North America. That this is not the sum total of the sort of societies or attitudes which Christianity has produced is also beyond question.

The Christian Gospel teaches that the world is purposeful, created and good. There is nothing in it which ought not to be, and there is nothing missing. But the Gospel also teaches that humanity has failed to live up to the role and position given it by God. This is captured in the myth of the Fall, Adam's failure to live as God had commanded. The Christian Declaration of Assisi spells out what this myth means today with regard to how we actually behave:

> *Christians believe that the first man's refusal to live according to divine wisdom introduced disharmony into his relationship with God and creatures, and this rebellion has perpetuated itself in history in various forms of social and personal injustice, dominion and exploitation, making it impossible for men and women to live in concord with one another and with the rest of creation.*

This both helps Christians to understand the roots of the obvious abuse of our world and also offers a hope:

> *But the heart of the Christian faith resides in its proclamation of God's merciful fidelity to himself and to the works of his hands. Christians believe that God the Father has not abandoned men and women to their sinful ways but has sent the Saviour to bring redemption and healing to everyone and to all things. Indeed they firmly confess that Jesus of Nazareth is the Son of God made man, that he is the fulfilment of his Father's covenant with Abraham for the salvation of all peoples and with Noah on behalf of all creation. They maintain that, risen from the dead and ascended into heaven in his glorified humanity, he recon-*

*ciles all things visible and invisible, and that all creation is therefore purposefully orientated in and through him towards the future revelation of the glorious liberty of God's children, when, in the new heavens and the new earth, there will no longer be death, mourning, sadness or pain.*

It is because of this hope, this belief that things can be reconciled and life lived more abundantly, that Christians can face the future and struggle to create a more just world.

As we have seen at various stages through this book, Christianity believes in a final End: the culmination of History and Time and the Judgment of the world. We have had cause to examine the perversions of this idea. But the true vision of a world without suffering, death, pain and loss is one which has sustained Christians down the centuries. The energies unleashed by Christianity's understanding of and hope for the world have been directed into actions of struggle for social, economic and environmental justice. For instance, in 1983, the World Council of Churches, a body bringing together more than 400 million Christians from all the major Protestant and Orthodox churches, launched a seven-year period of activity and study on "Justice, Peace and the Integrity of Creation", designed to assist its member churches in devising their own programmes of activity on these issues.

However, it has to be said that, until the secular world began to take up the issues of ecology, the churches had barely done anything to implement the ideas about caring for nature which lie nascent or dormant within the Christian scriptures and traditions. It has needed the spur of secular activity and criticism to stir the churches to take up the issue. In 1988, partly as a result of these forces, in particular the Assisi WWF meeting, the Vatican opened the first ever Pontifical Faculty of Christian Ecology to help train priests in awareness of the environment. It is only very recently that Christian development bodies have begun to look at the environmental impact of their aid work in third world countries. But now, for many schemes around the world, environmental impact is a key part of the studies before any development is begun, and environmental care is sought in the application of development.

But if secular conservationists have taught the Christian Church to look within its faith for the strength of vision to become again stewards of God's world, then the Church has also taught conservationists that ecology without justice and peace is no ecology at all. Too often, in the past, the conservation movement has actually ignored the human element. Often it has measured success by the extent to which it has actually kept local people out of its areas and schemes. At other times it has sought to work only through national governments to implement schemes of conservation. This has meant that many conservation projects have been dropped on local people without involving them, without their understanding, or against their wishes, by governments with a less than benevolent attitude towards their own poor and dispossessed. The inevitable consequence is that, in many countries, conservation has been seen as a white man's game; something for the tourists, but having nothing to do with the local people who have often been treated with scorn or resentment. They, in return, have come to view the game reserves or environmental policies as yet another factor in the oppressive regime under which they live.

The detrimental effects of this will be only too obvious. This is why the churches have insisted that ecology, justice and peace must work hand in hand—for what use is there in preserving an endangered species if the protectors are oppressors of their own people? Or what point is there in creating game reserves in an area where there is gross inequality in land ownership and use? Christianity, now predominantly a third world religion in terms of numbers, is able to speak with the people because, in many developing countries, it *is* the people. Yet the Christian Church also has access, because of its European, Western history, to the major decision-making bodies. So the Church is trying to engage not only in a re-examination of its own house and in seeking to set that in order, but also in voicing the words and fears, hopes and aspirations of the people.

## Hinduism

We have examined Hinduism in some detail already (see Chapter 3). We have seen how the sense of the divine spark in all life has

led to a respect of the right to exist and to a morality of *ahimsha*—non-violence. The attitude of *ahimsha* and the resulting code of vegetarianism, of reverence for life and of seeing all life as linked, contribute an important set of perspectives to the search for a wider environmental awareness. There is yet another contribution which Hinduism can offer: its willingness to leave questions hanging in the air, as a means of raising issues.

The term "Hinduism" was invented by outsiders. Legend has it that, confronted by the range of peoples, creeds, beliefs and cultures of India, Alexander the Great, looking across the river Indus, simply lumped them all together and called them "Hindus". The more likely source of the name is the Persian Muslim invaders, who likewise put all beyond the Indus under this one label. Hinduism, in fact, consists of a vast variety of beliefs, ranging from the devotional and personal to the questioning and at times atheistic. Let us now look at some aspects of Hindu thought. This is the opening hymn of the *Rig Veda*, probably the oldest of the Hindu scriptures:

*There was at first no Being—nor blank.*
*There was no air, nor sky beyond.*
*What was in it? Where?*
*In whose protection?*
*Was water there, deep beyond measure?*
*There was no death, nor deathless state,*
*No night, no day.*
*The One breathed without breath by its own power.*
*There was nothing else; no. Nothing else.*
*Darkness lay wrapped in darkness.*
*All was water, all, all over.*
*Love began, at first; desire was the seed of mind.*
*Sages and poets, searching within,*
*Saw the link of Being in non-Being.*
*But who really knows? Who can tell—*
*How it was born, where creation began?*
*The gods came later: Who then knows,*
*That from which creation came.*
*Whether founded well or not.*
*He who sees from heaven above.*
*He only knows. Or, He too knows it not!*

We may not expect to find in Hindu philosophy any practical help in our search for ways of caring for the environment. Yet here is made explicit something which is implicit in most other major faiths: namely, that we are ignorant; that what we make of reality is in fact illusion; that we can ask, but must never assume that we know the answer; that we may know, but what we know is but a fraction of that which is. Hinduism has sometimes been criticised by outsiders for being too passive, too accepting, too inactive. But this is to misunderstand completely one of the foundations of the Hindu perspective. As we have seen, there is no driving force of "once for all" mentality, either in the individual life or in terms of the overall life of the planet or the universe. It has all been before, and will be again. Furthermore, the idea that we "know" what to do also seems to many sadly laughable. Do we know? Can we ever know? And if not, then on what basis can we presume to act?

All that we "know" of the Divine is revealed in the beingness of all life. All life is, as we have seen, sacred. Therefore, we can see aspects of the Divine in various beings, just as we see aspects of the Divine in the various *avatars*, or incarnations, of the Divine as Vishnu, Shiva, Brahma, etc. To destroy any one of these manifestations is to attack the very nature of our own being: hence Hinduism's call to passivity, in contradistinction to aggressive, assertive action, and the reverence for all life.

To struggle for material well-being without spiritual well-being reveals, of course, an attitude of mind which all faiths condemn. Yet it is Hinduism which has constantly sought, along with Buddhism at times, to bring awareness of the physical/spiritual into the very active, knowledge-proud, materialist world of conservation. Dr Karan Singh, as the Hindu representative at the interfaith ceremony in Assisi which launched the network on conservation and religion, said the following, beginning with one of Rabindranath Tagore's poems:

*'Where the mind is without fear and the head is held high;*
*Where knowledge is free;*
*Where the world has not been broken up into fragments by narrow domestic walls;*

*Where words come out from the depth of truth;*
*Where tireless striving stretches its arms towards perfection;*
*Where the clear stream of reason has not lost its way into the dreary desert sand of habit;*
*Where the mind is led forward by Thee to ever-widening thought and action—*
*Into that heaven of freedom, my Father, let my country awake.'*

*This famous poem . . . postulates a state of inner freedom in which the human mind can develop its full potential without being distorted and constricted by rigid formulations. It beautifully expresses the Hindu concept that freedom, in the ultimate analysis, is an inner state of mind. . . . The basic concept of Hinduism is that the divine is both immanent and transcendent; it follows that the ideal human condition would be one in which all human beings are imbued with this awareness.*

Through this sense of the Divine in both the immanent and the transcendent, all of life, all of existence, is charged with the power and sense of the Divine. In Hinduism, the transcendent and the immanent are ultimately one.

*The ideal state, according to the Upanishads [one of the earliest scriptures], is one in which the power of the divine is seen in front and behind, to the left and to the right, above and below, and in which this entire magnificent universe pulsates with divine power. If this is achieved, then our life would undergo a fundamental transformation. The massive resources now being squandered upon weapons of destruction would then be released for furthering the welfare of all living beings. Each child born into this world would be assured of the material, cultural, intellectual and spiritual inputs necessary for a full development of their innate potentialities. . . .*

Hinduism's questioning of the progress-orientated, materialist model of understanding, which urges so many of us onwards but leaves us spiritually devoid, is perhaps its most important intellectual contribution to conservation thought. As we have

seen, there are also plenty of practical examples and attitudes springing from this which can act as a source of inspiration and challenge. But in the end it is the spirit of the creation hymn of the *Rig Veda* and the questioning attitude which allows no definition to simply stand, that perhaps offer the self-assured, all-defining, analytically reductionist Western world of today its greatest challenge and one of its greatest hopes.

## Islam

One of the most remarkable of all the Declarations of Assisi is the Muslim one, prepared by the Muslim World League. The League, which is based in Mecca, is the largest umbrella organisation for Islamic groups in the world, and represents the mainstream of Islamic thought. What is so remarkable about the Islamic Declaration is both the power of its vision of nature under true Islamic law, and its honesty about the failure of Muslims to live out this law in relation to the rest of creation. We shall look in a moment at the core doctrines of Islam with regard to nature, but let me just quote to you from the final section of the Islamic Declaration:

> *Muslims need to return to this nexus of values, this way of understanding themselves and their environment. The notions of unity, trusteeship and accountability should not be reduced to matters of personal piety; they must guide all aspects of their life and work. Shariah should not be relegated just to issues of crime and punishment, it must also become the vanguard for environmental legislation. We often say that Islam is a complete way of life, by which it is meant that our ethical system provides the bearings for all our actions. Yet our actions often undermine the very values we cherish. Often while working as scientists or technologists, economists or politicians, we act contrary to the environmental dictates of Islam. We must imbibe these values into our very being. We must judge our actions by them. They furnish us with a world view which enables us to ask environmentally appropriate questions, draw up the right balance sheet of possibilities, properly weigh the environmental costs and benefits of what we want, what we can do within the ethical*

*boundaries established by God, without violating the rights of His other creatures.*

This statement offers hope and a challenge. Firstly, it acknowledges that we fall short of the ethical values and beliefs which we espouse, but claims that we can nevertheless strive again to attain them. Secondly, it sees the tension between our secular roles and our religious beliefs and seeks a way of bridging these. Thirdly, it posits a belief system which is capable of delivering to humanity a complete way of life which would put us in a right and proper relationship with the rest of creation. Finally, it avowedly states that other creatures have rights. These are all very important insights for the world of conservation, even if some of them may prove a little difficult to accept.

The basis of Islam is belief in God (Allah is the Arabic word for God), the Creator who has revealed through the words of the various scriptures, and finally and completely through the Holy Qur'an, His will for all humanity.

*Behold! In the creation of the heavens and earth and in the*
*alternation of the night and day*
*are signs for men of understanding.*

*Such as remember God standing, sitting and reclining,*
*and ponder the creation of the heavens and the earth, and say:*
*Our Lord: you have not created this for nothing.*
*Yours is the Glory.*
*Preserve us from the doom of the Fire!*

(Surah III: 190–191 of the Holy Qur'an)

In these verses you capture the essence of Islam. God is the Creator. All life bears witness to this. Humanity has a special place, but it is to comprehend the Will and Purpose of God in creation and then to follow that Will. Failure to do so will lead to eternal damnation at the end of Time.

The Islamic concept of humanity's role on earth is very clear. We have been placed here as vicegerents of God. A vicegerent rules on his Master's behalf. He has no authority of his own, except that he has been chosen and endowed with responsibility by his Master. All final authority lies with the

Master and the position of vicegerent is held only on condition that the Will of God is carried out.

In Islam there are only two kinds of being who are endowed with the capacity of free will. All other creatures are, by nature, faithful to God's will, living in the way that He has decreed. But humanity and the jinns (spirits, usually mischievous or evil but also capable of being good) are given the power to decide for themselves whether to follow God's Will or to rebel.

> *Behold, your Lord said to the Angels: 'I will create a vicegerent on earth.' They said: 'Will You place there one who will make mischief there and shed blood, while we celebrate Your praises and glorify Your Holy Name?' He said: 'I know what you do not know.'*
>
> (Surah II: 30)

Islam takes the human-centred nature of Judaism and Christianity, but gives it a new dimension. Yes, all life has been created to sustain and support us, but we have to take responsibility for our actions. God has given us what is necessary for our daily needs. To take more than we need is to rebel against God. To waste what God has made is an act of blasphemy. The *Hadith*—stories and sayings of Muhammad—which rank second only to the *Qur'an* itself as sources of authority in Islam, contain many accounts of Muhammad setting an example with regard to right use of nature. He is depicted chastising those who torment birds for pleasure, those who waste food, those who squander water, those who ignore the needs of their animals. As one of the *Haḍith* says: "Created beings are the dependants of Allah, so the creature dearest to Allah is he who does most good to Allah's dependants."

At the heart of this is a vision of God as creator and thus provider for all life. All life is purposeful, because God has created it. Nor is its purpose found solely in its relationship to humanity. The *Qur'an* makes this clear:

> *There is not an animal that lives on the earth, nor a being that flies on its wings, but forms part of communities like you. Nothing have We omitted from the Book, and they all shall be gathered to their Lord in the end.*
>
> (Surah VI: 38–39)

God has created all life-forms because He wished to, and so that they could serve Him and glorify Him. And this includes humanity. It is within this understanding of life and creation that Islam spells out the responsibility of humanity to all life. The codification of this is found in what is known as the *Shariah*—Islamic Law. The *Shariah*, as developed over the centuries, spells out the consequences of Islamic belief. For instance, in the thirteenth century, the Islamic jurist Izz ad-Din ibn Abd as-Salam formulated a bill of legal rights of animals, based upon the *Shariah* tradition. Other legalists used the *Shariah* to ensure protection for water resources, to prevent overgrazing, to save forests and trees, to limit the growth of cities and so on. An example is the development of haram zones. These are legally proscribed areas around water-holes where hunting and trapping are forbidden so that all creatures can drink from the water-holes in peace. The *Shariah* contains some of the most important codifications of ethics of the environment that one could ever wish to encounter. It is a matter of great hope that Islamic jurists and organisations are now trying to unlock the vast resources of the *Shariah* in order to establish an Islamic *Shariah* of the Environment. If this can be established, then it will be binding on all devout Muslims and might help to bring about the change of direction and the application of Islamic values for which the Islamic Declaration of Assisi calls.

In looking at the contributions of Hinduism to the wider understanding of our world, I suggested that both the *ahimsha* element and the questioning, "reality is illusion" element were important. In looking at Islam, I would suggest that it is the organised, orderly and legal insights of the faith which present the most profound challenge to non-Muslims, as well as to Muslims of course! Islam sees itself as a way of life rather than a "faith" as such. Thus it legislates for all sorts of human needs and situations—including a proper use of nature. In the West we have a rather prejudiced vision of Islam. The sight of Islamic fundamentalists has soured our previously rather unhappy picture of the religion. Yet the vast majority of Muslims are not fanatics. They seek to live by a powerful and moving vision of the world and of God's purpose for it. "Islam" itself means "submission", a difficult word for many in the West. This is what the Islamic Declaration of Assisi has to say on the subject:

> *The word 'Islam' has the dual meaning of submission and peace. Mankind is special, a very particular creation of Allah. But we still are God's creation and we can only properly understand ourselves when we recognise that our proper condition is one of submission to the God who made us. And only when we submit to the Will of God can we find peace; peace within us as individuals, peace between man and man, and peace between man and nature. When we submit to the Will of God we become aware of the sublime fact that all our powers, potentials, skills and knowledge are granted to us by God. We are His servants and when we are conscious of that, when we realise that all our achievements derive from the Mercy of God, when we return proper thanks and respect and worship to God for our nature and creation, then we become free.*

Along with the ideas of submission and the special reasoning role of humanity in nature comes the concept of vicegerent (known as *khalifa* in Arabic). Because of the belief in the Judgment Day, there is also *akhrah*—which means Judgment. This Judgment will be meted out on the basis of how we have conducted ourselves, on the state of our khalifaship. Overarching it all is Islam's constant insistence on the Unity of God. The Assisi Declaration states the environmental consequences of such beliefs:

> *The central concept of Islam is tawheed or the Unity of God. Allah is unity; and His Unity is also reflected in the unity of mankind and the unity of man and nature. His trustees are responsible for maintaining the unity of His creation, the integrity of the Earth, its flora and fauna, its wildlife and natural environment.*

As vicegerents we have power over the rest of nature. But again, as vicegerents, we have our power only from He who appoints us. If we abuse our authority, we not only lose the right to have that authority but also we blaspheme against God who has appointed us to care for all nature on His behalf. As the Declaration says, Muslims have not always lived up to the teachings. This, of course, is true in all belief systems, but Islam was bold enough to admit it. And the Declaration goes on to make one of the most interesting statements of how environmental action follows from core beliefs:

> *So unity, trusteeship and accountability, that is tawheed, khalifa and akhrah, the three central concepts of Islam, are also the pillars of the environmental ethics of Islam. They constitute the basic values taught by the Qur'an. It is these values which led Muhammad the Prophet of Islam, to say: 'Whoever plants a tree and diligently looks after it until it matures and bears fruit is rewarded,' and 'If a Muslim plants a tree or sows a field and men and beasts and birds eat from it, all of it is charity on his part,' and again, 'The world is green and beautiful and God has appointed you his stewards over it.' Environmental consciousness is born when such values are adopted and become an intrinsic part of our mental and physical makeup.*
>
> *And these are not remote, other-worldly, notions; they concern us here and now. If you were to ask me what the notion of the Hereafter has to do with here and now, my answer might surprise you. I would say nuclear power and biotechnology. Both of these are very present here and now issues. Both have benefits and costs. Both have implications for the health and well being of mankind and nature. If I sincerely intend to be God's khalifa, His steward on Earth, then I must have an opinion about them, must prepare myself to make choices about them, because I will be accountable for what mankind has wrought with these devices in the Hereafter.*

## Judaism

Judaism has been studied, in part, in earlier chapters. The roots of Christianity and Islam and, indeed, of much of contemporary Western thinking lie in Judaism. Judaism's great strength is its distinctive style of debate and argument in which concepts and beliefs are arrived at through discourse. This is as true with regard to nature as it is with regard to God. The name "Israel" means, after all, "to struggle with God".

In the *Talmud*, the ancient and authoritative commentary on the *Torah*, the Five Books of Moses, there is the story of God and the angels looking at the world after everything except humans has been created. Then God decides to create Adam. The angels are distressed, and try to persuade God not to ruin his creation. They ask why Adam is necessary. God replies: "The birds of the air and fishes of the sea, what are they created for? What use is a larder full of delicious foods if there is no guest to enjoy them?" It is obvious from other stories, such as the one about the trees in the Garden (see page 99), that Judaism also believes that only fools would raid a larder rather than use and replenish a larder.

The notion of use of the wonders of creation is summed up in one of the more famous rabbinic statements, deliberately intended to make you stop and think. "He who denies himself any one of the rightful joys of this world is a sinner." The world is for us to enjoy. An unnecessarily mean or parsimonious attitude towards the permitted pleasures of the physical world is therefore cast, rather dramatically, in order to bring the point home, as a sin! This is meant to be debated, just as the image of the larder is meant to make you think about the balance between use and abuse.

Judaism is full of such images, often positing one point of view and then another. For instance, Genesis contains two creation stories. In one, the peak of creation is humanity, which is to subdue the earth. In the other, humanity is formed from the very dust, given life only through the breath of God and set in the Garden "to serve it and to keep it". This kind of tension runs through the Biblical and rabbinic witness to Judaism's relationship to nature. However, the core of Jewish belief about this is that God gave humanity authority over nature. And this brings with it responsibilities. When Adam is asked by God to name all the creatures (Genesis, 2:19), he is given tremendous power over them, for the power of naming is great both in the Bible and, if we think about it, in our own lives. If you know someone's name you can relate to them far more easily than if you do not. "Good morning, John" is a much more friendly and personal greeting than simply "Good morning". So in this we see Adam's power given by God. In the Kabbalistic commentaries (mediaeval mystical writings arising in Spain in the thirteenth century) we find that Adam not only gave the creatures their names, but also helped define their nature. At the end Adam is pictured as swearing to live in harmony with all whom he has named—a right and proper responsibility arising from the authority he enjoyed. But this proper balance of responsibilities was broken by Adam's disobedience and the resulting end of the time of Paradise. From then on (Genesis 4) we see Judaism struggling to find a restoration of the relationships. Through the Laws of Moses, temporal guidance was given for this. In the Book of Leviticus, the third of the Five Books of the *Torah*, comes the concept—the law—of the Sabbatical Year, whereby every seven years the land was to lie fallow, untouched by humanity. It was also a time when all outstanding debts were to be remitted; a time when relationships between peoples were to be set right. Likewise it was a time when relationships between the people and the land and the rest of creation were to be restored. The Bible commands that, just as, on the weekly sabbath day, not only the servants of the household but also the beasts of the household or farm should rest, so in the seventh year, the Sabbatical Year, the land and all creatures should rest. The wild animals should be allowed to enjoy the fruits of the fields and woods, unmolested, as part of the attempt to restore the relationships which have been disrupted by the disobedience of humanity. Leviticus 25:6–7 says:

> *And the Sabbath produce of the land shall be for food for you; for you and your servant and for your maid, and for your hired servant and for the settler by your side that sojourns with you, and for your cattle and for the beasts that are in your land, shall all the increase thereof be for food.*

In other words, you are to enjoy whatever the land brings forth of its own accord, and this is to be shared not just with your family, but with the stranger at your gate and with all creatures which live on your land, domestic and wild.

Fused to the Sabbatical Year idea is another fundamental insight which Judaism has brought to the world. In Leviticus 25:23 God says, "And the land shall not be sold in perpetuity, for the land is Mine." To this, rabbinic authorities added that the reason for the Sabbatical Year is that "God said to Israel, 'Sow six years and rest on the seventh so that you might know that the land is Mine' " (Sanhedrin 39a). The term "guest", used in the earlier story of the larder, begins to make more sense here. We are most highly honoured guests, dwelling by courtesy of the Lord on His land. To abuse or ruin that land, or the life of that land, would be to abuse the hospitality and thus to offend, particularly in ancient Hebrew understanding, against one of the most basic laws—that of hospitality. Leviticus 19:34, for instance, says: "If a stranger lives with you in your land, do not molest him. You must count him as one of your countrymen and love him as yourself—for you were once strangers yourselves in Egypt."

Judaism, of course, is particularly concerned with one land—the Promised Land. Furthermore, Judaism is not a proselytising faith, seeing no good reason why anyone other than Jews should have to bear the burden of responsibility which being a child of the commandments brings. Jews see themselves as standing before God on behalf of the rest of the world, and as bearing the moral responsibilities of the world, so that the rest of the world might continue. However, whilst Judaism has its 613 commandments which it is supposed to keep but which it does not seek to impose on the rest of humanity, there is also a message for the non-Jewish world. This consists of seven commandments which are binding upon all "the sons of Noah"—that is to say, all of humanity. Rabbi Arthur Hertzberg, vice-president of the World Jewish Congress, put this concept into its widest context, that of all humanity's relationship with all the rest of God's creation, during the interfaith ceremony at Assisi:

> *. . . from earliest times, the Jewish religion has insisted that the Bible has enjoined some basic moral codes for all humanity. (Sanhedrin 50–60). All people are descended from Noah. Judaism teaches that there are seven commandments which are incumbent on everyone. Amongst these seven laws are prohibitions against bloodshed and against eating the flesh cut from a living animal. . . . There is reason to believe that in the last centuries of Jewish independence before the destruction of the Second Temple in the year 70, these commandments were regarded as more than pious wishes. Rabbinic courts enforced, as law, the Biblical injunctions about defending the physical environment.*

Romantic environmentalists often turn to different faiths and cultures to find a "pure" attitude to nature which they can admire. Judaism stands as a severe block to this way of thinking. It uncompromisingly enjoys the physical world. It uncompromisingly sees the world as being for human benefit. But, at the same time, it sees God as being Lord of All and humanity as being in need of restoration to a proper relationship with God. It is the honesty of the Jewish witness, both to our tremendous capacities and to the dangers which abuse of these capacities brings, which makes Judaism such a vitally essential part of any consideration of conservation. Judaism holds us up as near equals to God and then throws us down to reflect upon our inhumanity. This is the tension of Judaism and it is a crucially necessary one. There is a story of three old rabbis in Auschwitz. They watch as their people are led away day by day to the gas chambers. The night before they are to die, they sit up all night and debate in true rabbinic fashion. Their question is, "Can there really be a God if He allows such terrible things to happen?" As morning breaks they conclude that, no, there cannot be a God. Then they kneel and say the *Shema*, the great prayer of Judaism, acknowledging God to be the Lord of His people and of the world. It is this kind of paradox which is so necessary to prevent religious thought on conservation becoming sentimental and thus incapable of engaging with the darker side of our nature. The Jewish Declaration sums up clearly some of the points mentioned:

> *And yet it must be said in all truth that this question of man's responsibility to the rest of creation cannot be defined by simply expressing our respect for all of nature. There is a tension at the centre of the Biblical tradition, embedded in the very story of creation itself, over the question of power and stewardship. The world was created because God willed it, but why did he will it? Judaism has maintained, in all of its versions, that this world is the arena that God created for man, half beast and half angel, to prove that he could behave as a moral being. The Bible did not fail to demand even of God Himself that He be bound, as much as man, by the law of morality. Thus, Abraham stood before God, after He announced that He was about to destroy the wicked city of Sodom, and Abraham demanded of God Himself*

*that He produce moral justification for this act: 'Shall not the judge of all the earth do justice?' (Genesis 18: 25). Comparably, man was given dominion over nature, but he was commanded to behave towards the rest of creation with justice and compassion. Man lives, always, in tension between his power and the limits set by conscience.*

## Baha'is

Finally, in this look at what the major universal faiths are trying to say and do in relation to the new awareness of ecological responsibility, we turn to one of the most recent of world faiths, that of the Baha'is. The Baha'is originated in Persia in the middle of the nineteenth century, around the figure of their prophet Baha'u'llah. They teach that all great religious teachers are part of the same path to God and that each is right for his time. Now Baha'u'llah is the prophet for our time. The Baha'is have been notable for their insistence on the unity of all humanity and for their support of those bodies, such as the United Nations, which seek to bring all peoples together. Their teachings are summed up in their central ideas:

*the Oneness of God;*
*the Oneness of Humanity;*
*that religious truth is not absolute but relative;*
*that Divine Revelation is a continuous and progressive process;*
*that all great religions of the world are divine in origin;*
*that their missions represent successive stages in the spiritual evolution of humanity*

The Baha'is now number over four and a half million members world-wide, but they are suffering terrible persecution, indeed virtual genocide, in their home area of Iran.

The Baha'is played a significant role at the WWF Assisi meeting, although they were not one of the main five faiths represented. However, within a year of Assisi, they had produced their own Statement on Nature. It is worth stopping for a moment to look at this happening itself. The Baha'is had never before publicly joined or committed themselves to a specific campaign involving secular and religious groups. But when they found themselves reflecting upon what they might have to say, following the Assisi initiative, they realised that ecology was an issue of such vital importance that they wished to join with others of good will. The entry of the Baha'is into the network on conservation and religion has been dramatic, for they have already started translating their ideas into action. In many countries in the third world, Baha'is have local development programmes running. These are now all looking to the environmental impact of their schemes and seeking ways in which they can be good for the environment as well as for the development of the area. The Baha'is are also launching their own internal education programme, as well as funding Baha'i specialists in ecology to be available for use by the wider conservation movement.

The Baha'i scriptures contain many moving texts bearing witness to Baha'i attitudes to nature. For example:

> *Nature in its essence is the embodiment of My Name, the Maker, the Creator. Its manifestations are diversified by varying causes, and in this diversity there are signs for men of discernment. Nature is God's Will and is its expression in and through the contingent world. It is a dispensation of Providence ordained by the Ordainer, the All Wise.*
>
> (Tablets of Baha'u'llah)

The Baha'i faith shares a basic outlook with the other "religions of the Book", namely, Judaism, Christianity and Islam. It sees God as creator and provider, and humanity as His highest creation so far—for Baha'is, arising in the era of scientific awareness, see evolution as the manifestation of God's will and believe that life is still evolving, just as the religious message to humanity is still evolving and progressing. What is missing from the Baha'i faith, as a member of the "of the Book" religions, is a sense of a terrible day of judgment. Instead, Baha'is believe that as we evolve, so we will achieve political and economic maturity. This will lead us to a situation where all will live, governed by one set of rules, as the inhabitants of one world. Caring for the natural world comes into this context. That we have not cared for it in the past is a sign of our immaturity. However, we are now at a crucial time where we know the path we could tread to greater unity and harmony, but are still in many cases trapped in the immaturity of our past ideas and actions. The Baha'i faith seeks to help humanity to maturity through the teachings of its prophet and through the witness of its members. The Baha'i Statement says:

> *While all religious traditions point to the kind of co-operation and harmony that will indeed be necessary to curb these threats, the religious writings of the Baha'i Faith also contain an explicit prescription for the kind of new world political order that offers the only long-term solution to such problems.*
>
> *'That which the Lord hath ordained as the sovereign remedy and mightiest instrument for the healing of the world is the union of all its people into one universal Cause . . .', Baha'u'llah wrote.*
>
> *Built around the idea of a world commonwealth of nations, with an international parliament and executive to carry out its will, such a new political order must also, according to Baha'i teachings, be based on principles of economic justice, equality between the races, equal rights for women and men and universal education.*
>
> (*The Baha'i Statement on Nature*, published by the Baha'i International Community, Office of Public Information, New York, 1987)

## The role of the feminine

One of the most interesting insights which the Baha'is bring to bear on the whole issue of conservation concerns the rise of the "feminine". They see the coming to equality of power of women as one of the most hopeful signs generally, and specifically for nature. As the Baha'i scriptures put it:

> *Man has dominated over woman by reason of his more forceful and aggressive qualities of both body and mind. But the balance is already shifting; force is losing its dominance, and mental alertness, intuition and the spiritual qualities of love and service, in which woman is strong, are gaining ascendancy.*
>
> (quoted in *The Baha'i Statement on Nature*, op. cit.)

Whilst not all feminists would agree with this statement, many people's feelings are borne out by the idea that, through a shift in world perspectives from the aggressive to the more feminine, nature would not be at such risk.

Likewise the Baha'i insistence on the vital role of education is important. We shall look at this in a little more detail in the final chapter. For Baha'is, the proper use of knowledge is crucial in the taking of responsibility. They welcome with open arms the discoveries of modern science. What they question is the way new skills are applied and the way new knowledge is used. For them, all actions should be under the guidance of God, and should be in pursuit of the true spiritual values of this life, not of material benefits.

The Baha'i witness is important because it embraces the world of modern science and the world of international, rather than national, politics. It tries to present a vision of where these trends could lead us. It lacks the sense of threat which imbues certain other faiths, colouring so powerfully their fears and their hopes. What the Baha'i faith tries to do is to construct a charter of maturity for a world which it sees as teetering on the brink of such maturity. It asks for our best, in a world which all too often seems only to be able to show either our indifference or our worst.

So the world is full of diversity. A multitude of perspectives, hopes, fears, lifestyles and cultures seek, each in its own way, to make the best of the world—in both senses of that phrase. What do we do with all this? That is what I want to look at in our final chapter.

# 5

# Not the End

*When the Present has latched its postern behind my tremulous*
*stay,*
*And the May month flaps its glad green leaves like wings,*
*Delicate-filmed as new-spun silk, will the neighbours say,*
*'He was a man who used to notice such things'?*

*If it be in the dusk, when, like an eyelid's soundless blink,*
*The dewfall-hawk comes crossing the shades to alight*
*Upon the wind-warped upland thorn, a gazer may think,*
*'To him this must have been a familiar sight.'*

*If I pass during some nocturnal blackness, mothy and warm,*
*When the hedgehog travels furtively over the lawn,*
*One may say, 'He strove that such innocent creatures should*
*come to no harm,*
*But he could do little for them; and now he is gone.'*

*If, when hearing that I have been stilled at last, they stand at the*
*door,*
*Watching the full-starred heavens that winter sees,*
*Will this thought rise on those who will meet my face no more,*
*'He was one who had an eye for such mysteries'?*

*And will any say when my bell of quittance is heard in the*
*gloom,*
*And a crossing breeze cuts a pause in its outrollings,*
*Till they rise again, as they were a new bell's boom,*
*'He hears it not now, but used to notice such things'?*

This poem, "Afterwards" by Thomas Hardy, makes a fitting start to this final chapter. For in the poem Hardy captures the enjoyment, awe and concern for the natural world which we have sought to explore in diverse ways through the different belief systems of the world. There is a sadness in the poem, a sense that the individual witness is but a brief flutter and is then extinguished:

> *. . . He strove that such innocent creatures should*
> *come to no harm,*
> *But he could do little for them, and now he is gone.*

Yet, by the very action of his trusting that people will recall that these things—the hedgehog, the hawk and so on—mattered to him, Hardy gives us a glimpse of hope. Perhaps what we do, and what we are, do make a difference after all.

## Soulless

In religious belief systems, death is never seen as the snuffing out, the End. More often than not it is seen as merely a stage on the road, or the start of real life. This does not detract from the concerns of living in the here and now, but it does provide a longer-term vision than a purely physical one, of meaning and purpose to one's existence. My children have a very "sound" book on the human body. It tells them, in nicely de-sexed pictures, all about growing up, puberty, sex, having babies, growing old and so on. Yet it lacks any soul. It cannot handle anything which is not strictly biological and thus it is ultimately useless for teaching my children anything about what they are. Anyone who thinks sex is simply a biological process is either celibate or in great emotional difficulties. Likewise the book's handling of death would be true farce if it were not for the pathos of it. As far as I can see, my children are expected to remember me by using my ashes to grow next year's roses in. The soul, the meaning behind the wonders of the physical beings called humans, is missing, and with it goes any possibility of actual understanding, any framework of meaning within which the physical can be placed and understood.

So it can often be with our attitudes to environmental problems. We cut out the soul, we deal only with the material, even reducing this to the purely economic. As I write this, a major British conservation body has brought out yet another report which tells us that the reasons for conserving nature are economic and human-centred—"We don't yet know if these plants will be able to help us treat AIDS or cancer." What a sad reduction of the powers of the Divine and/or the glories of evolution.

In looking at different belief systems, I hope we have been able to see that what we make of the material expressions of nature is coloured by what we understand the purpose of life to be and what meaning we see ourselves and the rest of creation to have. The sadness of the recent British report on conservation is that it betrays the motivations of its supporters. Hardy sounds a note which will strike a chord in many people's hearts. He fears for the world he loves because his is only an individual concern. Yet from such individual concerns have arisen the major conservation and ecological groups, seeking to combine the energies, wisdom, compassion and abilities of thousands who feel like Hardy. How depressing that such bodies then feel they have to be like the Devil they are combating—the Devil of the forces of environmental destruction—and use the language of the Devil and the power structures of the Devil. Conservation needs to rediscover the soul of the movement and the spirit which enlightens all of us. Religion needs to discover the true force of its insights and teachings and to find ways of harnessing its great authority and psychological power.

When we were planning the WWF event in Assisi, we found a number of themes kept recurring, albeit in different forms at times, depending on the different belief systems. From these I would like to share three, which, it seems to me, are crucial to an understanding of how we can relate the staggering plurality of beliefs about nature with the practical work of caring for or with nature.

## Celebration

The first of the themes is that of celebration, of thanksgiving. As we have seen, there is an extent to which the conservation and peace movements revel in depression, just as "blood and thunder" preachers do. The destructive forces contained within such a view, as well as its galvanising powers, have been explored earlier. What one rarely sees or senses is a simple joy at nature. There are notable exceptions, such as the wildlife films of, say, the BBC or Anglia Television. But it is rare for any conservation body to actually celebrate nature or to encourage or draw out a sense of wonder and reverence towards it. Assisi was a striking exception. Yet most people who care for nature do so for reasons not a hundred miles away from Hardy's feelings, or from those of the Australian aboriginals who sing of their land:

*Come with me to the point and we'll look at the country,*
*We'll look across at the rocks.*
*Look, rain is coming!*
*It falls on my sweetheart.*

There is a natural, and I use that word carefully, a natural delight in creation which expresses itself in many different ways. To cite one example which has deeply affected three major faiths and cultures, the Psalms are full of magnificent hymns of praise to and about creation.

In seeking a more holistic attitude to nature, no matter from what fundamental belief system we start, a sense of celebration, of joy and thanksgiving for what is, for what could be and for what we have received, is essential if we are not to become caught up in introspection and the anthropocentric view which sees purpose only when we need something. Through the new network on conservation and religion, various major faiths are developing within existing festivals, occasions for thanksgiving for nature. Interestingly enough, a number of zoos are also looking at ways in which they can have a day of thanksgiving for the wonders of nature. Recently, the British government, in line with other EEC governments, made grants available to farmers for returning land to the wild. Many farmers have wanted to use the opportunity of taking the grant and leaving land fallow, to express a sense of handing back to God that which has been held in trust. They have wanted to give thanks, to celebrate.

Celebration is a natural way of expressing the centrality and importance of something. Think of Christmas, Divali, Eid Ul

Adha or Purim. Through the cycle of festivals and the actions of celebration, key principles of belief and major symbols of meaning are brought to the fore each year and enjoyed. Currently we lack a sense of celebration in our secular manifestations of concern about nature, and perhaps the fusion of religious insights with secular knowledge can begin to make such celebration, enjoyment, possible. You cannot ask people to be earnest all the time. We all know the world can be dreadful. But we also know it can be joyful and full of surprises. Let the conservation movement acknowledge this, perhaps by fusing its concern with existing festivals, as the WWF in the UK is doing with the churches and Harvest Festival. In this programme, the joy at the fruits of the world—Harvest—is being fused with both a realistic assessment of the damage we have done and a celebration of God's Creation. From this arise wonder at creation; sadness at our destruction of nature; and hope with joy at the possibilities for change and action in order to care for nature.

Celebration is also an important acknowledgment of the "greaterness" of that which we celebrate. In celebrating what others have celebrated for years before us and which, God willing, others will celebrate for years after we have gone, we put ourselves into the continuum of life as but a part. It is a strange but powerful way of being actively passive! Much of our concern, especially in the West, is with what we do. In a festival or celebration we enjoy what is bigger than us, older than us, greater than us in every sense. What we celebrate does not need us, but we need it. Celebrations are sometimes dismissed as frivolous. They are, but they should not be dismissed as such, for we need to be frivolous to recognise that not everything depends on us. This is what I mean by "actively passive".

## Repent and recover

The second theme is one where I need to use two different terms. It is either the need for repentance, or the need to recognise our harmonising role. It depends which tradition you come from. For most people in the West it will be the need for repentance. I have deliberately put this in the middle, because repentance without thanksgiving is sin grovelling—that is to say, revelling in one's awfulness but never actually raising one's eyes above oneself as centre of the universe. Likewise, repentance without hope, our third theme, is to end up guilt-ridden—which is to end up fundamentally useless to man, beast and God!

In the right context, repentance can be immensely powerful as a healing and acknowledging process. All this talk about not wanting to destroy plants and animals because we do not yet know if they will be useful to us is a dangerous disguise for actually saying that we are responsible for genocide and for actions of appalling greed and destruction. For the sake of the rest of creation (and, quite frankly, forget about our own needs for a moment), we have to stop ourselves behaving like this. Appealing only to self interest is like building a first aid post outside a concentration camp. We need a far more radical challenge to ourselves than self interest can ever provide. We actually need to confess what a mess we have made. We need to stare our deeds in the face and to hear the cries of the dying world, of the slaughtered creatures, of the crashing trees and of the befouled seas.

Most important of all, we need to repent, not because our actions are harming us, but because they are harming other life-forms, part of the same web of creation which supports us and gives us meaning. And we need to ask forgiveness of the rest of creation. For in so doing, we acknowledge the "rights" of other life-forms, their importance and their sense of community, which we have for so long ignored, ridiculed or denied. Nor is repentance an individual action only. Organisations need to repent, especially those which consciously try to "do good". For instance, much of the Western conservation movement needs to repent of its arrogance, its racism, its cultural imperialism and its bigotry, for these have all led to failures of its greater purpose. An ability to learn from one's mistakes is probably more essential for major organisations than it is for individuals. And just burying the past does not mean that one has learnt, nor that one has restored broken or damaged relationships with others. Repentance for corporate sins and weakness is as important as individual repentance.

I used two terms in introducing this theme. "Repentance"

does not make sense within all faiths, because their perceptions of responsibility differ. Those faiths which posit a model of humanity as supreme under God, and therefore as having moral responsibility, need the concept of repentance in handling the issue of the destruction wrought by humanity. But faiths which see humanity's role as more integrated with the rest of nature have to cultivate a different way of handling the same issue. In these cases, the important thing is to re-establish the balance with nature. This requires critical examination of the extent to which a superiority model has actually infiltrated into the belief system and destroyed the concept of acting in harmony with nature. There must be, if you like, a calling back to fundamental principles and an abandoning or severely critical examination of those values which have begun to undercut the sense of participation. This might require, as in China, a public confession of failure and a return to older methods which are seen now to be more harmonious and healthy. It may mean a reworking of the myths, such as Hinduism is constantly undertaking, in order to find the models and the visions of understanding which can lead to hope for the world.

> *The dance of Siva is another perfect iconographical statement of ecology. What are his emblems? Agri, deer. What are his locks? They are the forests. Whom does he hide within himself? Ganga (water). And what adorns his hair? The sun and moon. What are his garlands? The snakes. And what does he wear? The tiger skin. And what does he bring to this world? The cosmic rhythm of his* damru *in the incessant process of cyclic creation, degeneration and regeneration and finally of enlightenment of knowledge wisdom by trampling upon the dwarf demon of darkness, ignorance, and finally he blesses with the gesture of beatitude of life.*
>
> (Dr Kapila Vatsyayan, *Ecology and Indian Myth*, published by All India Association for Christian Higher Education, Delhi, 1986)

Whether you think in terms of repentance or harmonising, this is a time of reflection about what has happened and about what must not happen in future. But, as I said before, this can only make sense if it comes between thanksgiving/celebration and hope.

## Hope

The final theme, therefore, is hope. Faiths, by their very nature, believe in the possibility of the impossible. They play with paradoxes in order to help us break out of believing that all that we observe is the sum total of reality, or even real at all. To use Christian language, faith believes in metanoia—the complete turning around of someone, his or her transformation from destructive to redemptive ways. In all faiths such a transformation is usually seen as costly, as involving the sloughing off of old comfortable ways and the making of new rules for one's life. Take, for instance, the king in the Jataka story of the golden deer (see page 120), or the story of St Hubert:

*Long ago there was a violent, aggressive and destructive knight by the name of Sir Hubert. He took pleasure in causing pain and distress to all God's creatures, both human and animal. He loved to hunt and was merciless in his pursuit of prey. He was proud and bombastic by nature, and terrorised the villages around his castle by his capricious behaviour. His servants and squires lived in dread of his temper, and few there were who counted themselves as his friend. Nor had he any respect for Christ or His Church. He rarely attended church and paid no heed to the attempts by the local clergy to calm his wildness or abuses of power.*

*One day he rose and decided to go hunting. His servants were aghast. For this was no ordinary day. This was Good Friday, the very day upon which Our Lord had been crucified and died for our sins. Surely today of all days Sir Hubert would not seek to kill any of God's creatures? But no: he was determined to have his way and the hunt made ready.*

*Through the castle gates streamed the pack with the hunters close behind. Soon they left the path and galloped across the meadows towards the forest. Then on the edge of the forest they caught sight of a magnificent stag who, hearing the baying of the hounds, turned and vanished into the denseness of the forest. But the hounds picked up his scent and were off. Behind them rode Hubert, with a fury such as few had seen before. Soon he had left his servants and squires far behind as he and his horse crashed on through the forest.*

*Hubert knew the forest well and saw that the hounds were driving the stag into a corner of the forest where sheer cliffs made escape impossible. With grim determination Hubert spurred on his horse. Sure enough, he saw the hounds turn towards the cliff face and he knew that through the next line of trees he would see the stag at bay. But what he actually saw shook him. For there against the cliff face was the stag. But instead of the hounds snapping and snarling at the beast, they lay motionless and soundless on the grass. Then, to Hubert's astonishment, his horse knelt to the ground, throwing the knight on to the turf. It was only when Hubert stood up and looked properly at the stag that he began to understand. For there, set between the great creature's antlers, was a crucifix. Hubert fell to his knees hardly daring to look upon this, the Golgotha of his own making; the Passiontide of his own anger; the evidence of his cruelty and sin.*

*They found him, hours later, still kneeling and praying. He wept as they carried him home, and for days he would not venture from his room. Then one day, like Christ from His tomb, Hubert came out. But this was not the old Hubert: for now he wore the simple gown of a lowly priest. He gave away all that he had to the poor and became in later years a great missionary. In churches dedicated to him his symbol may be seen: the symbol of how creation spoke for its creator—the symbol of the stag with the crucifix.*

(*Faith and Nature*, edited by Palmer, Nash and Hattingh, Rider, 1987)

All faiths have similar stories. They express a shared perception that that which currently obtains need not always be the same; old patterns can be radically transformed; the Divine can break through into the human with incredible results. The world can change, because people can change.

A major conceptual stumbling block for many coming at conservation from a secular angle is that they are fatalistic. They seem to believe that nothing fundamental can change. Perhaps this is because, by concerning themselves with the purely economic and material, they are never grappling with anything important enough to change. They are trying to sell the deck chairs on the *Titanic* rather than trying to change course. This fatalism is sometimes fed by those who see humans as entirely, or as good as entirely, conditioned by evolution and our given environment. They see no possibility of appealing to a higher value or purpose and thus are doomed to see the instinctive survival-of-the-fittest capacities of humanity leading us irrevocably to destruction. Religion does not and cannot accept this, for any belief in a power greater than one's self means that you can have recourse to ideas, models and aspirations which transcend—in all senses of that word—the given particulars of your own situation. That is where hope begins to make sense: hope in our abilities to be other than we are at present. This comes about with the breaking in to our lives of a sense of purpose, of meaning, which takes us beyond ourselves. Hubert is shown as experiencing this and all religions can bear witness to it in the transformed lives of many of their believers through the centuries.

Conservation uses the term "salvation" with great ease. There is much talk of "saving the world"—that is, of both saving it from us and our abuse of it, and saving it for those to come after us. Yet the true meaning of salvation is the fact of being freed from all that binds us and obscures our true understanding; and so it is a very dangerous and, at times, destructive force. It calls us to change and to break down the idols we have made of temporal things such as success, money and even comfort. Yet it also frees us to be fully human.

Hope is predicated upon a vision, and this is certainly where belief systems have much to offer to the ecological movement. Vision means an understanding of the forces which have shaped you, and of that within those forces which can be called on to shape a new future which makes sense. Vision is being able to see that things could be different, because of certain core beliefs which, if practised, could transform the present state of reality. Vision is also, in part, the art of forth-telling, often in story form, whereby that which is spoken of, Becomes—the word becomes flesh. Without vision, the people perish, as the Book of Proverbs puts it.

## Both walking and sitting

In all three of the themes discussed it is important to stress the interaction between action and contemplation. We are very prone in the West to stress the active side, and, of course, activist groups such as the peace movement or the conservation movement depend upon such energies. But much of our activism arises from a more quiet awareness which comes from being an observer, like Hardy in his poem, a celebrator of the world rather than just the organiser.

One way of participating in caring for nature, seen by many of the faiths, is to flow with, rather than to always struggle for or with. The *Tao Te Ching* quoted in Chapter 1 spells this out most clearly. Many of our belief systems see the world as essentially moving along its own natural path, and our role as being part of that movement. Things go wrong when we try to buck against the flow or to make ourselves masters of that which is, in truth, so much greater and so much more important than us. These beliefs result in a kind of trustingness, which is sometimes attacked as quietism, or passivity, by those who do not understand. This trusting is beautifully captured in these words of the fourteenth-century Christian mystic, Mother Julian of Norwich.

> *On one occasion the good Lord said, 'Everything is going to be all right.' On another, 'You will see for yourself that every sort of thing will be all right.' In these two sayings the soul discerns various meanings.*
>
> *One is that He wants us to know that not only does He care for great and noble things, but equally for little and small, lowly and simple things as well. This is His meaning: 'EVERY THING will be all right.' We are to know that the least thing will not be forgotten.*
>
> (*Revelations of Divine Love*, translation by Clifton Wolters, Penguin Classics, London, 1966)

## Of priests, prayers and people

In ICOREC's work with religious organisations beginning to respond to the conservation movement, we try to ensure both action and contemplation in each of three principal areas. These areas, where we believe each faith can contribute something distinctive both to its own believers and to those outside, are teachings—the great moral, spiritual and ethical insights into our world; liturgy, festival and myth—the great psychological forces which help us understand our world; and, finally, action, appropriate to each faith's own understanding and particular style. In each area the active and the receptive are equally important. And this can be said, too, in relation to the interfaith dimension of the conservation world, each faith being able to contribute something distinctive, but also being able to receive from other peoples and traditions, beliefs and values. When we issued the invitation on behalf of WWF to the world faiths, we asked them to come "proud of their own traditions, but also humble enough to learn".

So, finally, I want to leave you with something which has arisen in response to much that this book has tried to speak about. It is not an epilogue, for the last word lies with you and what you are, what you can become and what you will do. I hope that this final offering to you will be helpful, providing both a basis for reflection and an outline of action. It is simply known as the "Rainbow Covenant" and was launched on the first anniversary of the Assisi meetings, at the first Creation Harvest Festival jointly undertaken by the British Churches and the WWF. It is religiously rooted but designed to be used, privately or publicly, by all those of good will. It is based on God's Covenant with Noah, as recorded in Genesis 9. In that covenant, God promises never to wantonly destroy life again. The covenant is made with all creation, not just with humanity, as we saw in Chapter 1. The story then says that God set the rainbow in the skies, as a sign of his covenant and his promise.

Well, we know that God can be trusted to keep his covenant. But now it is we who are destroying life wantonly: we who are acting as though we were gods. And so we feel now is the time for a new Rainbow Covenant, between humanity and the rest of creation. When it was first used publicly to signify the willingness of the major churches and faiths in Great Britain to care for nature, it was sealed by the tying on to the wrist of one's neighbour in the cathedral at Winchester, of a rainbow thread.

This was made from seven strands of coloured thread woven together, symbolising the need we have for our neighbours to join us in caring with us. You may well be able to find other resonances of the symbol of the rainbow, revered in so many faiths around the world. The wording of the Rainbow Covenant is as follows, and you are invited to use it in whatever way makes greatest sense to you:

*Brothers and Sisters in creation, we covenant this day with you and with all creation yet to be;*

*With every living creature and all that contains and sustains you.*

*With all that is on earth and with the earth itself;*

*With all that lives in the waters and with the waters themselves;*

*With all that flies in the skies and with the sky itself. We establish this covenant that all our powers will be used to prevent your destruction.*

*We confess that it is our own kind who put you at risk of death.*

*We ask for your trust*
*And as a symbol of our intention*
*We mark this covenant with you by the rainbow.*

*This is the sign of the covenant between ourselves and every living thing that is found on the earth.*

In the end, it is up to each of us to look within ourselves and to see why we perceive the world the way we do and to judge whether this is how we want the world to be for us. At the same time, we need to look into the lives and witnesses of others, to see what strengths and weaknesses they highlight for us. Then, truly believing in ecology, believing in nature—and perhaps also believing in ourselves—and knowing what world it is we hope for, we can begin to move in order to be participants in the new world. Perhaps then we can begin to bring to fruition—as it is possible for human activity to do, in accord with the natural and the Divine—the vision of Mother Julian and of so many other saints and holy ones in history: that all can be well.

# RESOURCES LIST

The key resources which led to the creation of the alliance between the religions and conservation, and which have arisen from the new network, are the following:

*Worlds of Difference* by Martin Palmer and Esther Bisset, published by Blackies, Glasgow, 1985. This consists of an illustrated children's book, teacher's handbook and wallcharts published by Pictorial Charts Educational Trust. ISBN 0-216-91668-2.

*The Assisi Declarations*—five faiths commit themselves to ecology. Published by WWF International, Gland, Switzerland, 1986.

*The Assisi Liturgy*—the text of the interfaith ceremony which launched the alliance. Published by WWF International, 1986.

*New Road*—a quarterly magazine on religion and conservation published by WWF International and sent free to those requesting.

*Faith and Nature*, edited by Martin Palmer, Anne Nash and Ivan Hattingh, published by Rider (Century Hutchinson), London, 1987. Compilation of texts from eight world faiths on nature, plus prayers, wisdom, tales and a full description of the Assisi events. ISBN 0 7126 1921 6.

*The Winchester Liturgy*, published by WWF UK, 1987, and being a new eucharistic liturgy for conservation.

*Creation Harvest Service Booklet*, published by WWF UK, 1987. Readings, meditations, exegesis and hymn selections on the theme of creation in Christianity.

*Lord of Creation*, Easter meditations on Christianity and nature by Martin Palmer, published by Yorkshire TV and WWF UK, 1988.

*Believing in the Environment*, text of Environmental Education Lecture for the European Year of the Environment by Martin Palmer, published by the Council for Environmental Education, Reading, 1987.

Slide and tape sequences are also available from WWF International on the conservation beliefs of Judaism, Islam and Christianity—one set per faith.

WWF International's address is:
WWF International,
World Conservation Centre,
Avenue du Mont-Blanc,
CH-1196, Gland,
Switzerland

WWF UK's address is:
WWF UK,
Panda House,
Weyside Park,
Catteshall Lane,
Godalming GU7 1XR

Council for Environmental Education's address is:
Council for Environmental Education,
School of Education,
University of Reading,
London Road,
Reading RG1 5AQ

Other recommended books are:

*Tree of Life—Buddhism and the Protection of Nature*, by the Buddhist Perception of Nature Project, 1987, available through the coordinator, 5H Bowen Road, 1st Floor, Hong Kong. ISBN 962 7257 02 8.

*Towards a story of the Earth*, by Denis Carroll, published by Dominican Publications, Dublin, 1987. Excellent survey of traditional and new Catholic theology on nature. ISBN 0-907271 76 6.

*Environmental Crisis and Hindu Religion*, by O. P. Dwivedi and B. N. Tiwari, published by Gitanjali Publishing House, New Delhi, 1987. ISBN 81 85060 20 7.

*The Human Presence—an Orthodox View of Nature*, by Paulos Mar Gregorios, published by World Council of Churches, Geneva, 1980. WCC address: 150 Route de Ferney, 1211 Geneva 20, Switzerland. They also produce an excellent series of papers on ecology under the Justice, Peace and Integrity of Nature programme. Contact, Church and Society sub-unit, WCC.

*A Buddhist case for Vegetarianism*, by Roshi Philip Kapleau, Rider, London, 1983. ISBN 0 091 51971 3.

*Gaia—a new look at life on earth*, by J. E. Lovelock, published by Oxford University Press, Oxford, 1987 (with new preface). ISBN 0 19 286030 5.

*To care for the earth—a call to a new theology*, by Sean McDonagh, published by Geoffrey Chapman, London, 1986. ISBN 0 225 66485 2.

*The Future of Creation* and *God in Creation* by Jurgen Moltmann, both published by SCM Press, London, 1979. ISBN 0 334 00514 0 and 1985 ISBN 0 334 00571 X respectively.

*Creation and the World of Science*, by A. R. Peacocke, published by Clarendon Press, Oxford, 1979. ISBN 0 19 826650 2.

*Dove on Fire—poems on peace, justice and ecology*, by Cecil Rajendra, Risk series, World Council of Churches, 1987. ISBN 2 8254 0899 9.

*Battle for the Planet*, by Andre Singer, Pan, London, 1987. ISBN 0 330 29891 7.

*Our world, God's world*, by Barbara Wood, The Bible Reading Fellowship, London, 1986. ISBN 0 900164 69 7.

Useful addresses of environmental groups other than WWF and CEE given above:

Friends of the Earth,
377 City Road,
London EC1V 1NA

Survival International,
29 Craven Street,
London WC2N 5NT

Greenpeace,
38 Graham Street,
London N1 8LL

British Trust for Conservation Volunteers,
36 St Mary's Street,
Wallingford,
Oxfordshire OX10 0EU

For those wishing to join UK activities on religion and conservation, write to:

The International Consultancy on Religion, Education and Culture (ICOREC),
Manchester Polytechnic,
Didsbury Site,
Wilmslow Road
Manchester M20 8RR

# Index